GHOST TOWN
STORIES OF ALBERTA

GHOST TOWN STORIES OF ALBERTA

Abandoned Dreams in the Shadows of the Canadian Rockies

JOHNNIE BACHUSKY

VICTORIA · VANCOUVER · CALGARY

Heritage House Publishing Company Ltd.
#108 – 17665 66A Avenue
Surrey, BC V3S 2A7
www.heritagehouse.ca

Heritage House Publishing Company Ltd.
PO Box 468
Custer, WA
98240-0468

Library and Archives Canada Cataloguing in Publication
Bachusky, Johnnie
    Ghost town stories of Alberta: abandoned dreams in the shadows of the Canadian Rockies / Johnnie Bachusky.—1st Heritage House ed.

1st ed. published Canmore, Alta.: Altitude Pub. Canada, 2003 under title Ghost town stories. Includes bibliographical references.

ISBN 978-1-894974-72-1

    1. Ghost towns—Alberta—History. 2. Ghost towns—Rocky Mountains, Canadian (B.C and Alta.)—History. 3. Alberta—History, Local. 4. Rocky Mountains, Canadian (B.C. and Alta.)—History, Local. I. Title.

FC219.B22 2009   971.23   C2009-900133-0

Library of Congress Control Number: 2009920319

Series editor: Lesley Reynolds.
Cover design: Chyla Cardinal. Interior design: Frances Hunter.
Cover photo: Coal Valley, Johnnie Bachusky. Interior photos: Johnnie Bachusky, except page 53, courtesy of Bruce and Anne Vincent; page 71, courtesy of Lorraine Fraser; pages 60 and 91, photographer unknown.

Mixed Sources
Cert no. SW-COC-001271
© 1996 FSC
FSC

The interior of this book was printed on 100% post-consumer recycled paper, processed chlorine free and printed with vegetable-based inks.

Heritage House acknowledges the financial support for its publishing program from the Government of Canada through the Book Publishing Industry Development Program (BPIDP), Canada Council for the Arts and the province of British Columbia through the British Columbia Arts Council and the Book Publishing Tax Credit.

BRITISH COLUMBIA
ARTS COUNCIL

The Canada Council | Le Conseil des Arts
for the Arts | du Canada

12 11 10 09   1 2 3 4 5

Printed in Canada

For Ted (Larry) Bachusky
1950–2001

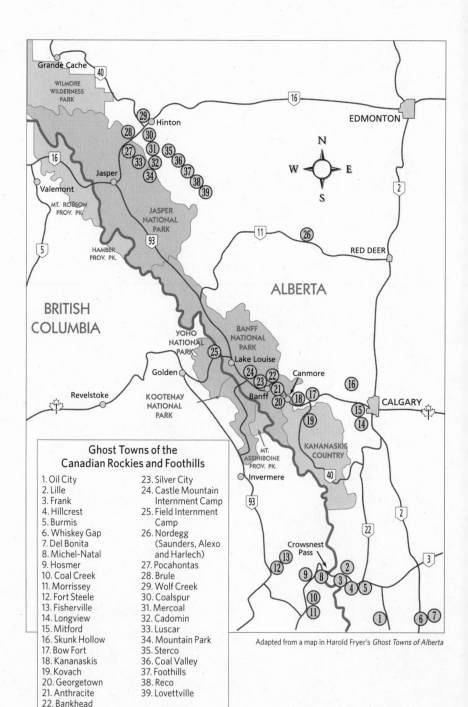

Ghost Towns of the
Canadian Rockies and Foothills

1. Oil City
2. Lille
3. Frank
4. Hillcrest
5. Burmis
6. Whiskey Gap
7. Del Bonita
8. Michel-Natal
9. Hosmer
10. Coal Creek
11. Morrissey
12. Fort Steele
13. Fisherville
14. Longview
15. Mitford
16. Skunk Hollow
17. Bow Fort
18. Kananaskis
19. Kovach
20. Georgetown
21. Anthracite
22. Bankhead
23. Silver City
24. Castle Mountain Internment Camp
25. Field Internment Camp
26. Nordegg (Saunders, Alexo and Harlech)
27. Pocahontas
28. Brule
29. Wolf Creek
30. Coalspur
31. Mercoal
32. Cadomin
33. Luscar
34. Mountain Park
35. Sterco
36. Coal Valley
37. Foothills
38. Reco
39. Lovettville

Adapted from a map in Harold Fryer's *Ghost Towns of Alberta*

Contents

Prologue

OCTOBER 31, 1941: ZUPI D'AMICO'S *shift in Nordegg's No. 3 mine was only two hours old when he felt an unsettling notion. A cold chill had swept through the veteran coal miner's soul. Something was not right.*

The details had not yet reached Zupi, but an explosion had just ripped through the lower level of the mine, and miners were frantically racing to the top, a desperate trek up a 900-metre slope. Thick coal dust was pouring out of the airways, choking every miner and horse.

Minutes earlier, Zupi, a young timberman, had felt the painful compression against his ears. It was a split-second, nightmarish, silent thunderclap, a horrifying sensation that signalled the very worst for any miner. It was followed first by silence, then muffled yelling several hundred metres away. Zupi and his crew stopped their work and bolted to the nearest airway to confer with others. They were told to investigate.

Zupi overheard a fire boss telling two miners not to worry and that it just might be a cave-in in a mine airway. "It's no airway cave-in. It's damn worse than that," said one of the miners. Less than a minute later, tell-tale thick smoke ended their efforts. It was impossible to go further. Time to get out. Time to think about living for another day.

Zupi could only imagine how bad it was. He noted the score of horrified and terror-stricken faces of miners racing up the slope with him. On the way up they met the shift manager, who was desperate for information. Zupi told him there had been an explosion. The shift manager then screamed, "Everybody get the hell out of here, get out of here, now."

Once at the top, the miners quickly headed to the lamp cabin. Zupi grabbed a safety lamp and headed back into the dust-filled mine with two others. The search for survivors began, but the miners were also wondering whether another explosion would doom their life-saving efforts. When the trio reached the district 900 metres below, a massive, grisly scene of death and destruction was spread out in every direction. There were bodies of miners and horses everywhere. Would there be any survivors? Zupi stared silently into the hellish haze. He had not seen his cousin Rudolph since his shift began.

The ultimate horror, every miner's worst nightmare, had begun.

Hopes and Dreams

"It isn't the telling of the history, it is the people. It isn't the buildings, nor the structures. They are just part of the weave. What really counts are the people, the hardships that they went through, the struggles."
—FRED LIGHTFOOT

IN THE FALL OF 1997, while working as a reporter for the local newspaper in the town of Banff, I met John Pearson, a retired cemetery supervisor in Banff National Park. John, it turned out, knew a secret.

In the 1960s, John was living in Anthracite, a former coal-mining community located eight kilometres north-east of Banff. Parks Canada leased a few employee residences at the site, on the south side of the Cascade River. An elderly visitor to Anthracite in 1965 told John a story she had heard many years earlier about a five-year-old child who drowned in 1883 while swimming in the river. The child was apparently buried across the street from John's place, under a towering Douglas fir behind a house.

Previous occupants of that house were said to have thought it was haunted.

John and his family left Anthracite in 1972—they were the town's final residents—but he never forgot about the secret grave. Twenty-five years later, when John was telling me this story, he said that all traces of his former home had vanished. The same was true for the house across the street. The only piece of evidence remaining from the woman's account was a small overgrown mound behind the spot where the "haunted" house once stood.

In 1997, John's speculations prompted Parks Canada to investigate. A team of archaeologists probed the site and declared the mound a "probable gravesite." A commemorative plaque was put up, becoming the first historical sign in Anthracite. John's disclosure breathed fresh life into the ghost town, shedding light on its once-thriving past.

Ghost towns in the Canadian Rockies share two main similarities. First, they were established because of coal, once the unrivalled king of Alberta's resource industry. From the Coal Branch to the Crowsnest Pass, coal ruled. Second, their populations were often on the move. When one mine shut down, the families just packed up and relocated to another coal-mining community. From Natal and Michel on the BC side of the Crowsnest Pass to Saunders in Big West Country and into Mountain Park, miners were one large family joined together by the lure of coal.

Many of the thousands of coal miners and their

A long-deserted road through Anthracite, a coal-mining community near Banff that died more than a century ago.

families who came to the Rockies were not prepared for the unforgiving hardships awaiting them. They faced isolation, natural dangers (such as rock slides and the threat of wild animals), primitive living conditions, weather extremes and even lawlessness. And always the miners knew that their lives could be snuffed out in a wink, so dangerous was their underground livelihood.

These towns also share some other similarities. One is that no ghost sighting has ever been confirmed (rumoured maybe, but not confirmed). Another is that there are no Canadian Rocky Mountain equivalents to the American wild west image of saloon doors flapping as a howling wind blows through a deserted town. (To see that, ghost-town hunters have to go west to the interior of BC or to some of the pioneer communities along Saskatchewan's famous Red Coat Trail.) If you want a picture of a typical Rocky Mountain ghost town, think of huge coal slags, concrete ruins and the remains of tipples and boiler houses. Two of the best examples of these towns are Hosmer, BC, and Bankhead, Alberta.

I have been asked many times to define the term "ghost town." My best definition is that ghost towns are former communities that are now shadows of their former selves. There is no need to expand on that, except to add that a ghost town does have to show signs of complete (or close to complete) abandonment. Perhaps the most visually intriguing Rocky Mountain ghost town is Lovett in Alberta's eastern Coal Branch. The townsite is filled with abandoned buildings, mostly wooden structures, bending and twisting from years of neglect and attack by the harsh elements. Lovett is about as close as it gets to meeting the traditional image of a ghost town. Unfortunately, it's also on private property and permission is needed from the owner to visit the site.

However, as Hosmer's Fred Lightfoot says, it's not the buildings or the structures that give a ghost town its mystique or its beauty. It's knowing something about the people who once lived there. This book describes the journey that many of those people took in making 11 Rocky Mountain communities—now ghost towns—their home. For the visitor who listens carefully, each one of these towns still rings with the sound of good times and bad, and reverberates with the memories of dreams fulfilled and dreams lost. In the end, though the people have moved on, these towns remain home to the spirits who once brought them alive.

The Day That Cancelled Halloween

HALLOWEEN WAS A JOYOUS EVENT in Nordegg during the tumultuous years of the Second World War. Even in 1941, the darkest year of the global conflict, there was a feeling of community spirit and celebration in the air that October 31. There were parties at school and evening trick-or-treating for students. And later, for the adults, there was the big dance at the Empress Hotel, known in town as the Show Hall.

This was a period of booming fortunes and good times in Nordegg, located deep in Alberta's Big West Country inside the eastern range of the Rocky Mountains. The mining company, Brazeau Collieries, could hardly keep up with the demand for coal. There was work for everybody, and coal miners from all parts of the province were rushing to Big West Country to be part of the prosperity. The town's population had almost hit 3,000.

Thirty years had passed since the first miners arrived in the area's rich coalfields. In 1914, the fledgling settlement opened its first post office, taking the name Nordegg after Martin Nordegg, the German entrepreneur who first staked his coalfields in this area of the Rockies. Nordegg wanted his town to be a garden paradise and designed it after the Montreal-area community of Mount Royal, with a wagon-wheel street pattern and imported European flowers. By 1941, the town had become one of the best-developed coal-mining communities in western Canada, with top-of-the-line sports facilities, a modern 19-bed hospital, churches and a three-storey, six-classroom school.

Anne McMullen was seven years old and in Grade 3. Like every other child in Nordegg that Halloween, she was looking forward to the day's fun. She headed off to school, saying goodbye to her father (known to everyone as Mac), a mining engineer in charge of the briquette plant. He was home being nursed by Anne's mother, Mattie, because of a work-related accident the week before.

Also looking forward to Halloween was 25-year-old Zupi D'Amico, though it was the dance, not trick-or-treating, that he was keen on. He and his girlfriend, Metha, had a date at the dance after his day shift in the No. 3 mine.

Zupi worked as a timberman, repairing wooden beams in the caved-in sections of tunnels where coal was dug out.

The morning of October 31, 1941, he went below as usual when his shift began at 8 a.m. The mine whistle, which could be heard by the whole town, screeched. It also blew at 4 p.m. and at midnight to mark the beginning of the other shifts. If it blew at any other time it could only mean trouble, likely fire or death.

The first hour of work went uneventfully for Zupi. He was fixing a cave-in with his brother Guido and three helpers. The night before, support timbers for the room had collapsed, leaving a messy pile of rock and wood. The five men were in one of two "districts" about 840 metres down the slope of the mine, at a depth of about 90 metres. The cave-in was at the base of a room located about 45 metres from the main tunnel. Upstream on the slope, about 150 metres away, was another group working in the main fourth level. The two districts were separated by an airway nearly 100 metres long. Below the fourth level was the fourth left water level, the bottom of the mine.

Shortly after 9 a.m., in Room 13 on the fourth left water level, two miners and a fire boss, Jock Armstrong, were preparing explosive shots to loosen coal. After drilling two holes, the miners plugged them with eight-pound sticks of dynamite. Jock ran about 30 metres of wire back from the dynamite and attached it to his battery. When an electrical current was released to the detonator, the dynamite would ignite. The men retreated behind a rock wall in anticipation of the explosions. In all, three shots were fired. One of the first two released a pocket of methane gas and highly combustible coal dust. The third shot ignited the deadly methane mixture.

At 9:12 a.m., Zupi felt the impact, a sudden change in air pressure against his eardrums. It was like a pair of hands suddenly being clapped over his ears. For that brief moment, he felt numb. He climbed across the room and walked 45 metres towards two miners meeting near an airway entrance. One of them, the fire boss in charge of his district, said a cave-in must have happened inside the airway.

"It was a damn sight worse than that," said the other miner. "There's something terribly wrong."

The fire boss dismissed notions of a serious explosion and ordered Zupi and the other miners into the airway to investigate. When they had gone only a short distance, they saw smoke moving their way.

Just before 9:30 a.m., the mine whistle blew, the first blast lasting at least several seconds, followed in quick succession by several short whistles. Housewives stopped to check their clocks. Early shoppers along Main Street paused. School children fell unusually silent.

In Anne McMullen's classroom, fear registered on every student's face. Many had fathers, uncles or brothers working in the mine. Ian MacQuarrie's father, for one, worked as a deep underground coal digger. So too did the stepfather of the teacher, Anne Pasechnik. A knock on the classroom door broke the silence, and the teacher went out for what seemed a long time. When she returned, she announced

19

that classes were dismissed. Anne McMullen left the school with her classmates. It was not immediately obvious to her what had occurred.

"Are you going out for Halloween tonight?" her friend asked as they walked home. Feeling uneasy, but still retaining some of the seven-year-old's faith, Anne answered, "Yes, I think so. Are you?"

"No, I won't be going out now, not after what happened," replied her friend sadly.

Nothing more was said. It was, however, the first moment that Anne realized that something was seriously amiss. Amid the unspoken fears, it was also clear that Halloween was cancelled.

Anne raced home. Her father, resting in the living room, was surprised to see his daughter back so early. "Something really bad has happened at the mine—really bad," she told Mac. "I have no idea what." Almost immediately, neighbours and friends started showing up at the house. News of the explosion at the mine had spread.

With thick coal dust pouring from the airway into Zupi's district, about 30 miners began moving frantically up the slope, collecting other men and horses as they made their way out. Halfway along, they met general manager Johnny Shanks. "Everybody get out of here!" he barked repeatedly.

Once at the top, Johnny told Zupi and another man to grab a safety lamp. The three headed back into the dust-filled mine to search for survivors. When they reached

The old bank as it looks today on Nordegg's Main Street.

the district, they saw a grisly scene of death and destruction. Eventually they learned that the explosion had killed every man and horse on the two lowest levels in the district.

They began the grim task of searching for bodies in the rubble. Among the dead were Zupi's 21-year-old cousin Rudolph and Nick Omelusik, teacher Anne Pasechnik's stepfather. Two brothers, Roual and Raymond Gervais, also perished. The three rescuers were joined by others, including the mine's official rescue team. Ian MacQuarrie's father, Hector, was one of them.

Jack Penman worked above ground as a trolley motor-man. He and his crew were unloading coal cars by the tipple

when they heard the news. The tipple was shut down immediately and Jack asked to help with the rescue. He was given
a different kind of task. "When the bodies are brought up,
they have to be washed at the wash house and then loaded
onto a truck," said the foreman bluntly.

For the rest of the day, 18-year-old Jack washed the bodies
of his fallen friends and watched as grief-stricken family
members came to identify them. The bodies were transported
to the Show Hall where preparations for the evening's
Halloween dance had ceased. The hall was now a temporary
morgue for 29 dead miners.

The entire town, remote and isolated from the rest of
Alberta, was in a state of shock. The mine closed for six weeks.
Classes were cancelled. Downtown streets were quiet. There
were no grief counsellors in 1941 to help the children cope
with the bereavement of losing loved ones or the enormity of
the town's loss. And there were no local papers or radio and
television news reports to offer any objective understanding
of the tragedy. Children learned only bits and pieces of
information by eavesdropping on adult conversation.

The day after the tragedy, Ian MacQuarrie and his
friends went to the Show Hall, where they heard the dead
were resting. The boys walked to the front entrance, but
were turned away. They tried a fire exit off the front deck,
but it was closed. Although shut out of the hall, they sensed
the grief everywhere around them. Ian was not allowed to
go to the funerals either. One was held later that week at his

church, St. Teresa's. When the service ended, he watched pallbearers loading the coffins onto a flatbed truck draped with black sheets. As the truck pulled away to take the fallen miners to their mass grave, he followed along. A huge crowd gathered at the gravesite. Ian stood at the back, listening to the speeches of union officials and friends of the deceased and to the sound of sobs and tears. Raised a devout Roman Catholic, Ian bowed his head and prayed for the dead men.

Almost six years later, in 1947, Hector began making plans to move his family away from Nordegg and the dangerous work of mining. He'd already checked out a few prospects on the West Coast.

On a lazy Sunday afternoon in June, Hector walked down to the local sports field to watch Ian play baseball. Hector was on his way to work at the mine, but had time to linger at the field for a while. He waved to his son and cheered from the stands. As the game progressed, Ian looked over once in a while to see whether his father was still watching, but Hector's shift forced him to leave before the end of the game.

Ian never saw his father alive again.

During Hector's shift, a cave-in seriously injured him and he died hours later in hospital. His funeral was at St. Teresa's. Ian was an altar boy at the service and he prayed again—and so too every day since.

The "Angel of Death" had knocked at the door
Of our secluded mountain and mining domain!
Twenty-nine miners were to answer that call!
The rest of the town, left in shock and in pain.
Each logging truck bearing some coffins,
Had a flat-deck all draped in black;
They whined out the mournful message,
"These miners are not coming back!"
The miners were laid to eternal rest.
Families since scattered like chaff.
All that remains in the ghost mining town,
Is our thoughts and a huge epitaph.

Mine Disaster, poems by Ian MacQuarrie (1998)

Jackpine Savage

SEPTEMBER 25, 1988. IT WAS another difficult night for Bruce Haack. He was in a deep depression. His hands trembled and he was perspiring heavily. He set the bedroom air conditioner on high. It was the only way he knew to help him sleep.

As he lifted his overweight body, wracked by alcohol-induced diabetes, onto the bed, he let his head drop like a stone onto the pillow. Bruce hadn't taken a drink that day, but was still feeling lousy from the night before and too many vodkas. At 57, the highly successful composer and artist—once hailing from Saunders, Alberta—was a physical and emotional mess.

Despite receiving critical acclaim over the past three

decades from some of the most important people in the US music industry, Bruce was sinking fast into the abyss. He was considered a genius for his innovative electronic children's music, yet he had not produced serious work since his 1981 landmark album, *Bite*. On this particular night, he just wanted those wretched feelings of unworthiness, loneliness and despair to disappear.

It was about midnight and Bruce's friend Ted Pandel had just left the apartment—a suite that Ted had added on to his home in West Chester, Pennsylvania, especially for Bruce. Since moving to West Chester in 1972 to teach keyboard music at the university, Ted had continued to take care of his long-time music-school chum and musical business partner. The two first met in 1954 at the Juilliard School, New York City's prestigious music academy. Ted hoped that bringing Bruce from New York to the more relaxed rural atmosphere of Chester County would help motivate him to get his life back together after years of drifting. It wasn't an easy arrangement, though.

"He put me through some hellish times," admits Ted. "When he drank, he was either terribly sad and crying, or berating whoever was around—and that was usually me."

Bruce was growing more and more dependent on Ted, who was always there for him on a moment's notice. He was also there to remind Bruce to get working again.

"Ted was the one who had the business sense. Bruce had absolutely none, and he didn't know how to sell himself," remembers Rita Pollock, Bruce's beloved cousin who grew up with him in Saunders. "As he got older and more sick and depressed, so did his music. His songs were not melodies you would walk down the street and whistle. It was heavy stuff, loud and grating."

According to friends, Bruce's chief escape when he was in a black mood was into the soothing memories of his childhood in the Rocky Mountains and in Saunders, the small coal-mining town where he was born in 1931.

Lying in the dark of his room that night in West Chester, it's very likely that Bruce was once more closing his eyes and escaping to Saunders and its surrounding pristine wilderness. The tiny community, which never had a population of more than 125 people, was located along what is now Highway 11 in the Big West Country, about 65 kilometres west of Rocky Mountain House. In the 1930s, this route was nothing more than a bumpy dirt trail—and about as unlike New York City's rat race as could be possible.

Saunders was one of several Big West Country coal-mining towns (along with Nordegg, Alexo and West Saunders) that began in the area along the dirt trail staked by German entrepreneur Martin Nordegg in the early 1900s. These communities lacked many of the normal amenities of the era, but the wilderness offered residents a wondrous refuge. Bruce, for one, adored the breathtaking alpine vistas all around the town, the wild animals, the eagles soaring high overhead. With Rita, probably his closest childhood friend, he would tramp in the bush for hours, his Boston bulldog, Beans, at their side.

Bruce also liked to recall the "jackpine savages" he'd known. That was the term local folks gave to mountain bush people. And there was a particular man in Saunders whom Bruce liked to remember—a grizzled illegal immigrant from Russia named John Harbonovitch—who was the epitome of a jackpine savage. John was a machinist at the mine and he lived alone in a cabin near Saunders Creek. The mine workers knew "Big John" as a hard worker and (with most of his after-work hours spent at the local hotel) as a hard drinker. Women ignored him and children regarded him with fearful fascination.

"John really scared us one night," says Dorothy Kay, a Saunders schoolmate of Bruce's. "He was drunk and for some reason had come to our back porch and was trying to get in the house. He was so drunk he didn't know where he was. One of us snuck out the front door and went running for help. Someone came and pulled him off the porch and took him home. It frightened us because we were just kids."

While Big John may have been the subject of countless whispered conversations in town, he proved to be a valuable resource to members of the tiny community. During the hungry Depression years, when there was very little work at the mine, most residents survived on garden vegetables, wild meat and fish from the North Saskatchewan River. Near his cabin, Big John discovered

Big John's Spring is one of the few historical reminders still remaining at Saunders. It was named after John Harbonovitch, a mine machinist who built the structure in 1932 to serve as a cooler.

a way for townsfolk to keep their food and water supplies fresh. A pathway ran from his cabin to the creek. One day in 1932 while out walking, Big John discovered water seeping from a side hill. He climbed up a bit and dug a hole.

As water began flowing into it, he realized he'd found a spring. He built a little shed around it to create a cooler. People stored perishable food there, and whenever the mine's washhouse water line froze up, Big John allowed folks to help themselves to water. Over the years, it became a regular sight to see residents walking along Big John's path from the creek, loaded up with as many buckets of water as they could carry.

Unfortunately for Big John, his wild ways were his undoing one very cold winter night in 1944. After an evening of heavy drinking at the hotel, he staggered home and collapsed in an alcoholic stupor on his doorstep. Though he managed to pull out his house key before falling, he passed out before he could unlock the door. He froze to death where he fell, with his dog at his side.

Even at the peak of his career in New York, Bruce never forgot the stories of Big John, and he used Jackpine Savage as his pseudonym for his 1971 album, *Together*. That project was an electronic pop work, intended to move him away from his established career as a composer of children's music. Nevertheless, many of the whimsical lyrics still celebrated his childhood.

In truth, however, while Bruce relished his Saunders roots and jackpine savage memories, his childhood had not been completely without demons.

Bruce's father, Clark, was the local mine accountant. He was generally a grim, cheerless and even frightening man.

Crippled and deformed by childhood polio, he ruled his house strictly and ruthlessly. Bruce's equally stern mother, Bertha, was constantly bedridden with a variety of ailments, though she somehow found the resolve to control every facet of her son's life. This was especially true when it came to music. She forced Bruce to spend most of his after-school time practising the piano.

The Haacks left Saunders when Bruce was five to live in Rocky Mountain House, where Clark and Bertha ran a variety store. Bruce kept up with his music, giving piano lessons and playing in country-and-western bands.

"Bruce was the centre of his parents' universe, but they were very critical and sarcastic, not only with him, but with everybody else," says Rita. "When they were in Rocky [Mountain House], they were grooming him to be a concert pianist. I used to get letters from him that he wrote on the bus going from Rocky on a Saturday morning to Red Deer for a music lesson. He had very childish handwriting, and he'd always start his letters with an apology to his parents for being such a bad son."

About the time Bruce left Rocky Mountain House to attend university in Edmonton in the late 1940s, Saunders was in decline. The mine closed down in 1952 and within a few years the last resident had left. Saunders became a ghost town. Today, half a century later, only a children's cemetery remains to remind visitors of the once busy little community. The cemetery contains about 10 graves, all of children who were born in the early 1930s but died either at birth or from influenza. Unknown to official government registries and bureaucrats at the time, the children's remains were lovingly placed in makeshift coffins constructed by a mine carpenter and buried here near the bank of the North Saskatchewan River.

Dorothy Kay's younger brother Arthur is buried in the cemetery. He had been a twin and died when he was little more than a month old. Shortly after the small family funeral service held for him, locals found the baby's seven-year-old brother, David, by the grave with a shovel in his hand. "It was so sad," explains Dorothy. "David couldn't understand why they had buried the baby down there. He was going to dig him up." Dorothy is planning to make the children's cemetery her final resting place too.

Even after moving away from Saunders, Bruce often thought about the cemetery. Depending on his frame of mind, according to Rita, Bruce would feel either lucky or cursed to have been one of the Saunders babies who was born in the early thirties and survived. On that September night in 1988, lying in his room in West Chester, he may well have been wondering about those children—and if so, he was probably feeling cursed.

In the early sixties, Bruce teamed up with Esther Nelson, an accomplished American children's dance teacher. Together the two produced children's works that were educational and open-minded. Along with Ted, they started their own record label, Dimension 5. Bruce's music defied definition with its innovative mix of country, medieval, classical and pop. Although he had little formal training in electronics, he made synthesizers and modulators out of any gadgets and surplus parts he could lay his hands on, including guitar effects pedals and battery-operated transistor radios. He even created instruments capable of 12-voice polyphony and random composition. Important names in the entertainment industry began to take notice. Bruce appeared on television shows such as *I've Got a Secret, The Mr. Rogers Show* and *The Tonight Show with Johnny Carson* (where he played the Dermatron, a touch- and heat-sensitive synthesizer, on the foreheads of guests). His work was innovative and fresh, but it did not rocket him to fame and fortune. The shy, insecure man hated being on stage and was a nervous wreck before every concert or television appearance.

"Bruce was not that well known," says Ted, "even though he was tremendously influential. Part of that was his own making. He was very reclusive; you had to push him."

However, everything Ted had tried through the mideighties to help Bruce turn his life around was meeting with failure. Bruce's depressions were getting progressively worse. On that September 25 when Ted visited Bruce in his suite, he didn't stay long. After almost 35 years of friendship, he knew better than to try to coax Bruce out of a depression.

The following morning as Ted left to go to work, he

looked up at Bruce's window where Bruce usually stood, waving him off to work. That morning Bruce was not there. At 4 p.m. when Ted came home, he phoned up to Bruce's suite, but got no answer. An hour later, he went up and knocked on the door. When still he received no response, he went in. There on the bed he found his old friend, dead.

Bruce had passed away in the early hours of September 26, 1988. The cause of death was heart failure. He was buried in a rural cemetery in West Chester.

For many years while living at Ted's, Bruce had written to Rita about his adopted home. His poignant descriptions of the countryside nearby reminded her in many ways of Saunders. It would seem that despite his considerable success, Bruce—the gentle jackpine savage—never really strayed far from his roots in that beautiful and remote Alberta landscape.

Hockey Night in Mountain Park

MIKE PAVICH WAS A PROUD Mountain Park rink rat. Many times after an evening of public skating, the arena custodian cornered him and his friends, Pete Chiesa and Eddy Bracko, to scrape off the rink's leftover snow. The 10-year-old never hesitated.

Rink ratting in 1940 was an honourable means for Mike and his friends to save the 15 cents admission fee to get in to the Sunday hockey game, which usually attracted crowds of 200 or more. It was the golden age of hockey in Mountain Park, and the Sunday game was the place to be. It was an event that defined a Coal Brancher's passion.

One time, when a powerful Edmonton senior team roared into town, the Mountain Park Arena was packed with almost 500 rabid fans, pulling in an unheard-of $200 in gate receipts. The game ended in a tie and everybody went home happy—especially after hearing how the Edmonton team had clobbered Mountain Park's Coal Branch rivals Cadomin and Luscar on the same road trip.

If Mike and the boys weren't picked to rink rat, they stooped—literally—to any level to get inside. The lads would meet at a prescribed time at a secret wooden panel on the outside of the rink. They'd pull up the panel and then, one by one, crawl in like commandos to the foot-high space separating the ground and the arena floor.

"We'd get dirty down there, but we didn't care. We *had* to get in," says Mike. Their entry was timed at just a few minutes before the game started. As the boys crawled forward inches at a time, they'd hear the noise of the crowd overhead. Along the way, pieces of straw would get stuck to their clothes, faces and hair. By the time they covered about three full metres, they'd be a mess, looking more like unkempt barn cats than impish mine rodents. At the exact right moment, they'd pop up through an opening into the arena and slip into the crowd, hoping that custodian Frank Liverio wouldn't catch them.

The arena was bound to be filled with a charged and loyal crowd, especially if the game was against the town's arch-rival, the Luscar Indians, a team perennially in pursuit of the provincial championship. Often the rink rats found themselves watching Jim Bello, a diehard hockey fan whose two sons, Ellio and Melio, starred for the senior Mountain Park Provincials team. Jim was instantly recognizable by his signature close mustache and deep voice that shook the rafters with every syllable. He sat at his special place on the bleachers, a blanket around his knees and smoking a big Italian cigar. He roared with every play and was always getting after his boys for not playing hard enough or smart enough.

Mountain Park was a rough-and-tumble coal-mining town lying under the shadow of the towering mountain peaks of Jasper National Park. From 1911 until 1950 when both the mine and town closed, Mountain Park—situated at an altitude of 1,908 metres—was the highest inhabited community in the British Commonwealth. At its peak, the multicultural community grew to a population of 1,400 and included citizens of more than 30 nationalities. It was also considered one of the most remote and inaccessible places in Alberta. Outside people generally thought civilization ended at Cadomin, 13 kilometres north, especially in the winter when the only way to get to Mountain Park was by train.

The spectacular alpine countryside offered locals ample summer recreational opportunities, including fishing, hunting, rock climbing, hiking and horseback riding. Winter was another story, since at any time one of the region's infamous metre-deep snowfalls could occur, immobilizing the town for weeks. When that happened and no one was able to ski or toboggan on Mount Harris or Flag Pole Hill, hockey action at the arena could always be counted on.

Prior to 1932, hockey was played outdoors. Despite what were often harsh weather conditions, locals and out-of-town hockey enthusiasts packed the perimeter of the rink. The fortunate ones huddled together on open-air bleachers; standees pressed together like upright fur-wrapped Popsicles, their numb hands buried deep in their overcoat pockets and their wind-chilled faces and ears mummified in thick, tightly wrapped scarves. During the games, the goal judges stood behind the nets and the referee rang a bell instead of blowing a whistle to stop and start play.

Not even the worst blizzards and coldest sub-zero temperatures could halt the growing popularity of the game. This near-fanatical interest did not go unnoticed by management at the Mountain Park Coal Company. The firm wanted bragging rights to the best hockey team in the Coal Branch, and it competed aggressively against other coal-mining towns to ice the best players.

Even before the Second World War erupted, company brass was bringing in talented players and semi-pros such as Wilf Shaw, Peter Elock, Rudy Bobrosky, Alex Watt, John Wayda, Al Patrick and Bill Green. "These guys got a job at the mine, with the most important prerequisite being that they could play hockey," says Frank Lovsin, a former senior-league player in Mountain Park. "There are stories told about slopes being driven into uneconomic coal seams just to keep the hockey player miners working."

While the company worked hard in the backrooms to

get the best hockey talent, the local miners were ultimately responsible for the toughest assignment: building a decent indoor rink—and even funding it out of their own pockets. Mountain Park Coal agreed to lend the miners money to build their rink of dreams. Every worker was then deducted $1 per paycheque to pay back the loan. As well, every miner was required to volunteer three eight-hour shifts or pay an equivalent of $15 towards the final cost.

When the new facility was finished in 1932, Mountain Park residents boasted about what they believed was the biggest and finest hockey arena west of Edmonton. Located near a ravine along the McLeod River, the building included an ice surface 25.5 metres wide and 55.5 metres long. There were also two dressing rooms, a common room, two sheets of curling ice and custodian living quarters.

Almost immediately, the Mountain Park Arena became the place to be in the town. It was the winter social hub—not only for Mike Pavich and his rink rat friends, but also for the miners and their wives. In the summertime when there was no hockey, curling or winter carnivals, the arena was used for weekly movie nights. It's even remembered as the scene of a bizarre party that took place in September 1934. The Cheviot Hotel caught fire, but townsfolk were helpless to save it. Hundreds of locals gathered around and watched the blaze—all except a few thirsty miners.

"Some of them went to the bottom floor of the hotel and took out kegs of beer. They cheerfully rolled them down the bloody hill to where the arena was," says Joe Voytechek, one of Mountain Park's most celebrated senior hockey players. "The miners simply sat down on the kegs, drank their beer and watched the hotel burn."

But as winters came and went, the most memorable heat was on the ice rink, especially in the late 1930s and into the early 1940s. Before 1940, Mountain Park had several top local teams, including the Hawks, the Elks and the Flyers. Shortly after the war broke out, another new senior team was formed. A local contest was held to pick the squad's new nickname and crest. Willy Graham, a 16-year-old local boy, won with his suggestion, the Mountain Park Provincials. His winning entry earned him a season's ticket to all Provincials home games. According to Mike, Willy said to him years later, "You know, when I think of it now, that was a silly name. I was thinking of the province. But a provincial is sort of a hick guy, a country boy."

The "Provincials" may not have sounded as menacing as the "Hawks," but when the arch-rival Luscar Indians came to town, there was nothing hickish about the local boys. They played with spirit.

The rink rats were always pumped up for Luscar. They were also in quiet awe of the out-of-town players, who were legends across Alberta. Twice during the 1930s, the Indians won the Provincial Senior Amateur Championship, including a sensational come-from-behind series victory in 1936 over the Coleman Canadians. That series ignited interest across the province, notably from Edmonton because many of Luscar's top players, including Lindsay Carver, Eddie Shamlock and Leo Lemieux, originally hailed from the capital city.

"The Luscar Indians rose to great heights in turning in a spectacular victory before a capacity crowd of more than 4000. It was really a brilliant win for the northern Coal Branch team," gushed the *Edmonton Bulletin* newspaper. "They earned it by cool and deliberate play under heavy fire, and are worthy champions of the province for the second time in three years." In 1940, the Indians were still the team to beat. And two years later they once again rose to glory with another provincial title.

Whenever the Indians came to town, Mike and his friends parked themselves in front of the arena. The Luscar star players included Mike Onychuk, a big, slick centre who dominated the ice like NHL Hall of Famer Jean Beliveau, and Claude Bartoff, the team's superb goalie who was renowned for wearing a leather football helmet on the ice.

"We loved to watch them come in. The Luscar guys were so tall, big and cool. They wore dress pants, fedoras and team jackets. They looked so professional. We had our mouths open. We were like kids at a rock concert," recalls Mike.

When the games started, it was fire on ice, Mountain Park style. Besides Nino Chiesa, Joe Voytechek and the Bello boys, they had formidable players in big defenceman Eddie

Harrison, goalie Billy Lancaster and forward Les Marshall. Lancaster was a crowd favourite, a streetwise, scrappy teenager who played the net with daredevil nerve. He and Chiesa, as locals revelled in telling visiting fans, even entered the bucking bronco event at the Mountain Park rodeo in the late 1930s. Marshall, for his part, reminded fans of the legendary Montreal Canadiens forwards Maurice "Rocket" Richard and Howie Morenz.

With the rivalry fierce, Mountain Park players desperately wanted to dethrone the Luscar team. Tempers and fights often flared up. "It was a tough league," admits Joe Voytechek. "There were times when the Provincials went to Luscar to play hockey in the back of big coal trucks. We would load them all in and, as you can imagine, it would get colder than hell. But they couldn't always get the truck up the bloody mountain to reach Luscar, and the players would spend most of the time shovelling snow. When they finally did get there, they'd play a period or so, and it wasn't unusual for a hell of a brawl to break out and the game to be called."

By 1944, Mike had to give up rink ratting. He was 14 years old, in Grade 9, and growing too big to crawl under the arena. Besides, he had his own hockey team to play on— the bantam-level Mountain Park Grizzlies.

During May of that year, a late spring snowstorm started hammering most of the Coal Branch. Snow in May was not unusual for Mountain Park. However, it was soon to become

The cemetery at Mountain Park, as it looks today.

the worst storm since 1917. By May 24, about 140 centimetres of snow had fallen on the town. The Canadian National Railway branch telegraph line was broken in 50 places and 35 power poles snapped under the weight of wet snow.

The following day, everybody at school was talking about the storm. Still, that did nothing to prepare Mike for what he saw later that day after school: the collapsed roof of the arena. He was devastated, as was pretty well the whole town. Just the week before, the last deduction had come off miners' cheques to repay the coal company's 1932 loan for building the rink.

The rink would never be rebuilt. Not only was there no

insurance, but rumours were already afoot in 1944 that the mine was in financial trouble.

Mike played with the Grizzlies on an outdoor rink for a few more years until he and his family left Mountain Park in 1947. Although it was the same rink—only uncovered, as before—hockey in Mountain Park was never the same. The rink rats lost their home, but never their memories of that Sunday game beside the McLeod River ravine, in the highest hockey arena in North America.

As Joe Voytechek sums it up, "For us who played hockey in Mountain Park in those years, we were as close to heaven on earth as we'll ever be."

A Love Story

IN THE 1950S, IN THE male-dominated coal-mining town of Mercoal, Alberta, there was no way a man should accept a paycheque from a young immigrant woman with a Grade 8 education. There was no way that banks should ever consider giving such a woman a business loan either, despite an impeccable credit rating, or that she should ever own and operate a successful car dealership, even though her well-respected family had run it for years without a hitch. There was just no way. But then again, Amelia Spanach was no ordinary woman.

Ernie Foss recalls meeting Amelia at the train station in 1931, when she and her mother, Mary Pankovich, first arrived in Mercoal. Amelia was just five; Ernie was seven.

Amelia's father, George, was a friend of Ernie's dad, and the three of them had gone to the station to pick up Amelia and Mary. "They couldn't speak any English," remembers Ernie, "and Amelia was shy."

George had come to Canada from Yugoslavia in 1927, the year after Amelia was born. Once established, he'd sent for his wife and daughter. When Mary arrived in Mercoal, the first impression she had of the new country filled her with disappointment. That Canadian autumn was especially cold, and snow was already blanketing the rugged Alberta Coal Branch community. The gloom of poverty was everywhere as the Depression years took hold. The only available house for the family was a renovated two-room chicken coop without electricity.

With work slow at the coal mine, George bought a cow and a few chickens to help feed his family. Mary started making her own cheese, cream and butter. By selling the eggs and a little bit of milk to the mine bosses and workers, she raised money to buy coal oil for their lamps and shoes for the family at 75 cents a pair.

During Amelia's first years in school, she was often teased and taunted. She spent many days in class crying. "Kids being kids, they pointed at me and laughed because I was different. It was humiliating," Amelia now recalls.

She was also prevented from enjoying any after-school activities, including sports. George and Mary were old-fashioned and set in their ways. They believed the role of young girls was to cook, sew and help at home. Nevertheless, Amelia quickly learned English and then helped another Yugoslavian family with four children to speak it.

She slogged through school to finish Grade 8, but then it was back to doing housework. Only daughters and sons of mine managers and pit bosses were able to go further in school, because their parents were better paid.

There may have been no dances or skating parties for her throughout the 1930s, but as the decade came to a close, Amelia, now a pretty young woman, was about to see her life change. One day Mary sent her daughter to the Mercoal Mercantile to buy some lemons. Amelia was not yet 16. When she entered the store, a handsome man was standing by the wood stove warming himself. Amelia had never seen him before.

The man's name was Bob Spanach and he was 27 years old. Another Yugoslavian, he had come to Canada in 1928 and now owned a lumber business in Luscar. His early years in Canada, without family or friends, had been lonely and poor. He'd spent his first months in the new country jumping onto one train boxcar after another, going from farm to farm, mine to mine, looking for work. He finally landed in Luscar, working in the coal mine.

Bob supplemented his mine income by cutting timber in the bush. Eventually, when the mine companies' demand for timber increased, he was able to start a planer mill at Steeper, a railway whistle stop a few kilometres uphill from Mercoal.

On the day Amelia was sent for lemons, Bob was in Mercoal to scout out badly needed timber for use in the mines. He and Amelia exchanged glances. She hurriedly purchased her lemons and left the store. After she'd gone, Bob asked the clerk who she was. He was only told that Amelia's mother sold milk and eggs.

For the next two months, Amelia's family had a new regular customer, a man who travelled to Mercoal, across the Coal Branch from Luscar, to buy milk and eggs. Of course, it wasn't just coincidence that Amelia was always at the house whenever the gentleman arrived. By 1941, Bob had finally gathered the courage to invite Amelia to Luscar to see a movie. Her parents flatly refused to permit it.

"After the first refusal, I snuck off. We were taking our chances," says Amelia. "By this time, we both realized we wanted to get married. But I was also worried about how I was going to get my parents to allow me to marry him. In those days, a girl was brought up in the old European way. You didn't do anything that your parents said you couldn't do."

The young, lovestruck couple went to a movie, but there was a storm waiting for them when they got back to Amelia's house. Bob was assailed by the elder Pankovichs for dating their daughter without permission. The young lumberman stated firmly that he loved Amelia and wanted to marry her.

A huge argument erupted and Bob left the Pankovich home. It was now up to Amelia. "I had a big cry and said to my mother, 'If you do not let me marry him, I am going to run away and do it.' I even threatened them that I would go and work for him in one of his camps," says Amelia. "That was the worst thing I could have said, but also the best because they started to worry that I might."

Amelia and Bob were married on August 24, 1941.

With the Second World War going on, times were prosperous everywhere in the Coal Branch, including Mercoal. Demand for both coal and timber was high. Bob expanded his lumber business, employing about 200 men at the peak. He was supplying lumber to the mines in Mercoal, Luscar and Mountain Park, as well as to the railroad companies. He opened the Mercoal Café, a 12-room boarding house, a theatre, a gas station and Mercoal Motors, a General Motors dealership. Along the way, he and Amelia had three children, Mary (who died as a child of complications from a spinal condition), George and Diane.

Although Amelia had had a rigid European upbringing, she was not restricted to the role of traditional housewife. Quite the opposite: she blossomed into a real partner for Bob. While he was often away in the bush, she looked after the affairs for his huge crew of truck drivers, handled office duties and met the trains that brought in supplies, groceries and parts. Her English was also improving. In fact, it was always more advanced than Bob's and he relied on her for his correspondence.

It was a good time to be in Mercoal. The mine, owned by

Canadian Collieries Ltd., was running at full capacity, with up to 250 men on the payroll and coal production jumping to 1,200 tonnes a day. The population of the community mushroomed to nearly 1,000. During the early war years, another Mercoal entrepreneur, John Kapteyn, expanded his beer parlour and added a walk-in cooler. He doubled the size of his hotel to 40 rooms and built an 82-seat café. His neon "Hotel and Café" sign was the first of its kind in the Coal Branch.

Amelia and Bob's businesses were also booming, and the couple was well respected by the community. "Bob was an absolute prince of a guy. He donated lumber for the Elks Hall, legion and the curling rink," says Ernie Foss. "Gas was rationed in those days of the war, but when I wanted to go to a dance, Bob never turned me down when I asked to buy some."

After the war came ominous signs that Mercoal's future and the couple's financial prospects were not to remain as rosy as they'd been. In 1947, Bob's garage, which serviced his truck fleet and equipment, burned to the ground. The following year, the first mine layoffs were announced at Mountain Park. There were worries throughout the Coal Branch that the arrival of diesel fuel spelled doom for the coal industry.

Bob and Amelia, however, were already planning their next business move. In 1948, with the company's affairs too complex for them to handle, they hired an office manager, 26-year-old Steven Cheer. Bob started putting out feelers to sell his Mercoal operations and in October 1949 he sent Steven to Edmonton to look into opening up a lumberyard. But a different kind of change was about to take place.

On October 25, while Bob was out visiting his mill in Steeper, a piece of equipment broke down and the mill temporarily ground to a halt. When workmen finally started up the machinery again, Bob was standing too close and one of his sleeves got caught in an equipment belt, pulling him into a saw. A worker quickly stopped the machinery, but not before Bob was crushed. He was taken to the first-aid station at Mercoal and an ambulance was called.

Bob was still conscious when Amelia and other family members got there. "That was the last time he spoke to me," says Amelia. There was nothing that could be done to save Bob. At the age of 23, Amelia was a widow. The mine shut down for the day of Bob's funeral, and the town mourned the death of the kind, generous Yugoslavian.

Amelia's life was shattered by grief. Still, she couldn't retreat for long. There were two children to raise, employee bills to be paid and businesses to run. Once again Amelia turned her back on the social standards of the day. She decided she was going to pull through, whatever it took.

It was nearly November and time to get men into the bush to work. However, because Bob had not left a will, all of his assets were seized by the public trustee and held for his two children. Amelia could not touch a cent. To keep the Spanach businesses afloat, she had to find a lender. With much effort, she finally managed to secure a $10,000 loan from a family friend, one of the few sympathetic bank managers she encountered over the next quarter century—but the public trustee was always watching over her shoulder.

Next, she went to several different insurance companies to try and borrow money so that she could purchase her children's shares from Bob's estate. It was not easy. "Because of my age and the fact I was a woman, they laughed at me," says Amelia. "I'll never forget two fellows who asked me, 'What are you doing in this lumber business? What is a woman like you doing this for? Why don't you go out and get married?'"

Eventually, Steven Cheer, who had stayed on in Mercoal to assist Amelia, helped her get a $50,000 loan from Canadian Collieries Ltd., which she used to buy out her children. Over the next decade, Steven continued to help Amelia through every hoop and around every obstacle imaginable.

When the banks and public trustee were not throwing up roadblocks in Amelia's way, other businessmen were, even the ones she had thought were loyal family friends. Like sharks in a feeding frenzy, many began to undercut her to get Bob's contracts.

It was no better outside the Coal Branch. Within a week of Bob's death, a General Motors official came from Edmonton to say that the company did not believe a woman could, or should, run a garage and sell cars. Amelia was forced to sell

This 1942 aerial view of Mercoal shows the town and mine.

Steven the Mercoal dealership, with a side agreement that the business was owned by her.

There were other reminders, too, that it was a "man's world." Steven recalls how one of Amelia's male employees came into the Mercoal office to remind him it was still 1950. "He told me, 'I never worked for a woman, I do not intend to, and seeing as there is a woman here, I do not want to accept a cheque. I will not accept pay from this woman.'" The only way for Amelia to keep moving forward with her businesses was to give her father the responsibility of paying the men.

"She was very determined. She wanted to keep going,

same as Bob did," says Steven. "Many times she would come to the lumber camps with me and go all over the place—to where the men were cutting logs, to the cookhouse, everywhere—and she would listen to them."

Amelia fought and struggled in Mercoal for the next decade. There were always new challenges to face. In 1956, a forest fire destroyed the mill. She borrowed money to build another. Three years later, the town's mine closed and most of the residents left. Amelia had to lay off all her employees and close her businesses. Within a couple of years, Mercoal became a ghost town.

In September 1959, Amelia moved to Edmonton to start a new business, Spanach Construction Company. It was the same old story in the capital city—a woman in business raised eyebrows.

"I was applying for a bulldozer contract with the city," she recalls, "and was told I needed a licence for the equipment. When I went to city hall and said I'd like a licence for a cat, I was sent upstairs—for a kitty cat licence. So I went back downstairs and I told the guy, 'I am looking for a Caterpillar licence.' He eyed me and asked, 'Is that for yourself?' I answered, 'Yes.' Then he said, 'I thought ladies looked after kitty cats.' 'No,' I replied, 'they look after bulldozers too.'"

Amelia retired in 1976. Under the leadership of her son, George, the company was still operating proudly under the Spanach name into the 21st century.

A Love Story

Amelia never remarried. Every October, on the anniversary of Bob's death, she puts a memorial notice in the *Edmonton Journal*. In 2002 it read:

> What I would give to grasp his hand, his happy face to see, to hear his voice and see his smile that meant so much to me. If all this world were mine to give, I would give it yes and more, to see my loving husband come smiling through the door.

"Every time I was falling down, I kept thinking of the struggle Bob had," says Amelia. "For example, in the summertime he would have a few men cutting logs. When he was going to see the men, he always wanted to take bread. I would stay up all night and bake that bread. If I couldn't finish it, I'd ask my mother to. I just couldn't let him down."

Jokerville

MARIA LOVENUIK DID NOT LIKE it when people called her dad the Joker, and her mother resented being called Mrs. Joker. But her father, Nicholas, didn't mind one bit. He was a prankster and proud of it. His gentle teasing of others was his way of helping new arrivals relieve the anxieties they felt when they first came to Coal Valley, a wilderness coal-mining town along the eastern line of Alberta's Coal Branch.

Laughter was also a soothing safety valve for Nicholas. It was the thing he especially needed after a tense day's work at the coal mine. He was a blasting foreman, the position most people knew as the "powder monkey." Not that the job was a joke. It was dangerous work. But when a work day was done, Nicholas always sought laughter. On the way home, he invariably found his mark for a good chuckle.

Nicholas loved people, and he had a generous heart. Many times during the Depression years, he would greet his family after work with hungry house guests in tow. Sometimes they would even stay the night.

"There were bums back then who used to ride the rails," recalls Maria, "and my father often brought them home. He gave them an axe and had them chop wood. Then he'd feed them. Sometimes we kids would have to give up our beds."

During the early years of the Second World War, there were times in Coal Valley when intolerance and paranoia were rampant against anyone in the community who didn't fit the majority's idea of who was truly Canadian. Many of the Lovenuiks' neighbours were immigrants. Nicholas himself was Russian and his wife, Anna, Polish. Both sometimes felt the sting of being different, but Nicholas' zest for life never wavered. He kept things light. In fact, the wisecracking powder monkey from the mine became so popular that his section of town in Coal Valley was dubbed Jokerville.

Coal Valley was one of four main communities located a kilometre or two apart on the remote stretch of the Rocky Mountain foothills where entrepreneurs first began staking the rich coalfields in 1907. When the Coal Branch railway arrived in late 1912, a mining town named Lovett (Mile 57, as many called it) was already in full operation. The railway line quickly became known as the Lovett Branch. Within a few short years after the First World War, coal exploration moved northward up the Lovett Branch and several more mines and towns got up and running. They included Reco at Mile 52, Foothills at Mile 50, Coal Valley at Mile 48 and Sterco at Mile 47. The close proximity of these communities to one another mitigated the isolation that residents felt from the rest of the Coal Branch and beyond. For almost three decades, the only way in and out of the Lovett Branch communities was by rail. Although a few automobiles were shipped in on rail flatbeds during the 1930s, it was not until 1941 and the opening of the Burma Road between Sterco and Coalspur that the Lovett Branch towns were connected to the rest of the Coal Branch by motor vehicle traffic.

Coal Valley, meanwhile, became the vibrant hub of the Lovett Branch. With its own electrical power, indoor plumbing and sewer system, it was considered to be one of the most modern coal-mining towns in Canada. It was also a community where up to 75 percent of the population was French-Canadian and Roman Catholic—including mine president Charles Barry and his wife, Annette. (Not surprisingly, perhaps, the residents of the elite section of Coal Valley, known as Uptown, were mainly French-Canadian.) Schoolteachers in the town were even required to be bilingual.

Although Coal Valley's population never exceeded 300, the town had three distinct neighbourhoods: Uptown, with the well-off folks; Jokerville, or Downtown, where Nicholas

L

)

The townsit
that had d
mining

t

dr

the n

home. She foun

of windows and dragged in

think he ever played the game again.

Life in Coal Valley was almost always chan

new arrivals. When Nicholas and Anna first came to the
town in 1930, they built their own log and mud house. However, wilderness living was just one hurdle. Anna remembers being upset when children threw snowballs and stones
at her because she couldn't speak English.

When the Second World War started, discrimination
and taunting had to be endured by most members of the
Jokerville community. During the early war years, times
were particularly hard for Russian immigrants, and more so
when their native country attacked Finland. Often they were

...e of Coal Valley, an eastern Coal Branch community ...ed by 1960, along with several other nearby coal-...ommunities.

...alled derogatory names such as Doukhobors, Bohunks and communists.

But the Russians weren't alone in being the target for patriotic hysteria. During a raucous town meeting at the community hall on June 27, 1940, those citizens present unanimously agreed to ask the Coal Valley Mining Company not to hire any "enemy aliens" or enemy sympathizers while the war was going on. The crowd also wanted the company to fire all currently employed enemy aliens and sympathizers and to allow only British subjects to hold senior mine positions. The same crowd even agreed to ask the company to deny employees the right to speak any language other than English or French.

If the paranoid turbulence generated on the home front by the war wasn't enough, Coal Valley's minorities also had to contend with a small but very nasty group of racists festering at the fringes of the town's life.

Romeo Piquette, who lived in the Uptown neighbourhood, recalls a cross-burning one summer in either 1939 or 1940. "I guess there were a few Ku Klux Klan supporters just on the outskirts of Coal Valley on the hill. From our house, I saw a glow on the hill behind the tipple. The next day I went out with my brother to see what it was all about. We saw the burnt cross on the ground. Tin cans with fuel in them had been nailed to the upright post and the cross arms. My dad said there'd been a few KKK people around before. He wasn't pleased about it."

While the Klan flared up briefly in Coal Valley and other Coal Branch locales, interest wasn't widespread, and fortunately for the town's minorities, the group's activities died out.

Nevertheless, that incident and the patriotic hysteria were unsettling for the Lovenuiks and other Jokerville families. What really disturbed Nicholas was that by 1940 he had been in Coal Valley for a decade, a fact that seemed to matter little to some nationalist zealots. Not that he let this tension stop his love of a good joke. Nicholas' immigrant neighbours were only too happy to have a reason to laugh.

"I think Jokerville was a closer-knit community than Uptown," says Maria. "Everyone there came from different parts of the world, but they all had the same problems. They were all in the same boat."

Jokerville children, however, did not worry themselves over their parents' hang-ups or the trials of the day, and they mixed quite freely and cheerfully among all of Coal Valley's neighbourhoods. One of the main reasons for this relative harmony was the town's one-room school in Uptown. Here, hostility and discrimination were far less played out because so many of the young people came from other parts of the world and other parts of Canada. The building in which the children attended school was also the hub for most of the community's social activities. A truly multi-purpose facility, it also served as the church, the town hall and—best of all in the minds of many—the theatre.

"It cost 10 cents for kids and 25 cents if you were older. The theatre was where we saw all those Wild West movies," Maria remembers fondly.

Roland Piquette, Romeo's father, was the theatre manager and projectionist. He was a short, wiry man, but amazingly strong. Everyone called him "Husky." A tipple worker by day, he would rush home after his Friday mine shift for a quick supper and then head to the theatre to set up for the Friday and Saturday evening shows. It was an important part of the week for many residents along the Lovett Branch, who eagerly walked down the road from Sterco and Foothills to catch the latest movies that had just finished a first run in Edmonton. Husky also ordered newsreels for the 35-millimetre projectors. These were especially important to residents during the 1940s. Television had not yet arrived, and radio-station signals from Edmonton were unreliable. Every week, Husky provided movie patrons with 20 minutes of the latest news footage on the ongoing battles in Europe and the Pacific, as well as on women's activities in the war effort and updates of the aircraft industry.

Romeo believed he was the luckiest kid in Coal Valley. As the movie man's son, he got to see every show for free. On weekday evenings, he watched his dad at home typing letters to movie distributors, ordering films and paying the bills. He also went down to the train station with his dad to pick up the movies. When classes ended on Friday, Romeo and his classmates shoved all their desks under the stage to clear the space for the weekend movie nights.

During the shows, Romeo's job was to rewind the reel. His dad had to keep careful watch of the projector because it heated up during each film, threatening to burst into flames at any second.

When the Saturday evening film finished, Romeo helped set up for next day's church service. Benches were rearranged and the hall's large sliding doors opened for the altar. On Monday morning, students retrieved their desks from under the stage and their classroom was ready. It was a Coal Valley routine that everyone knew well.

Besides films and Nicholas providing Jokerville residents

with a distraction from problems in the outside world, Coal Valley had animals that seemed to play that role too. If Coal Valley had had a newspaper, it's a safe bet that animals would have been a regular front-page feature.

The Kukuchkas' cantankerous rooster, known to attack without provocation, was one example. Every time kids on bicycles rode by the Kukuchka house in Jokerville, the rooster bolted out of nowhere and began pecking at legs. Former locals swear that many young kids set peddling speed records during their encounters with the feisty bird. Then there was the friendly moose that arrived every winter. It took a strong liking to members of the Kukuchka household. The family placed a little bell around its neck and it became a colossal-sized pet for everyone.

Bears were much less friendly and in fact were almost a daily problem in Jokerville and throughout Coal Valley. Again it was the Kukuchka home—or, specifically, the Kukuchka chicken coop—to which the bruins were drawn. Once, a grizzly bear became too threatening in the schoolyard and had to be shot. Another time, when Peter Kukuchka was fishing with his dog a few kilometres outside Coal Valley, he found himself between a mother black bear and her two cubs. He dropped everything and climbed a tree. On his way up, the bear managed to bite down on his foot. All he was wearing on his feet were rubber boots, and the animal's teeth tore right through and deep into his ankle. Peter pulled out his pocket knife and poked it in the bear's eye. The dog, meanwhile, was attacking the bear from behind. Finally, the bear had enough and left. Peter climbed down the tree and commanded his dog to go back to town. Within a few hours, a group of Jokerville locals arrived and Peter was helped home.

Maria Lovenuik left Jokerville in 1945 to go to high school in Edmonton. Nicholas the Joker and Anna stayed on until 1953, after which they also moved to Edmonton.

By 1960, all the communities along the Lovett Branch, including Coal Valley, had become ghost towns, victims of the declining demand for coal and the growing demand for oil and gas. One by one, each mining town was given over to black-dusted phantoms.

When Maria took her six-year-old son on a visit to Coal Valley during the 1960s, the only residents left were Peter and Stephanie Kukuchka, who had stayed on as caretakers of the ghost town. Maria recalls being heartbroken at seeing the loneliness and emptiness that had overtaken the place. Her house was gone, as was most of everything else that had been in Jokerville.

While she mourned with the Kukuchkas the vanishing of her former home, she noticed her son playing on a swing, one of the few remnants of the old neighbourhood. It was then, remembers Maria, when she caught sight of the boy laughing and smiling as he played, that her mood shifted slightly. The spirits of Jokerville and her past, she realized, were perhaps not all that far away.

God-Forsaken Places

WILLIAM (BILL) WARDILL LOOKED A little worn out and, here in this place, a little dazed. With a friend, the 74-year-old had just hiked five kilometres from a trailhead beginning at the west end of a residential street in Canmore. The well-maintained hiking path had taken them through dense forest and up to this alpine clearing on the lower southeastern slopes of Mount Rundle. Above the clearing, they continued along another trail to where Bill's friend pointed out a crumbling cement foundation just to the south of the path. The ruins were almost invisible against a tangled maze of tree stumps and broken branches.

"This," Bill declared, "is a God-forsaken place."

Bill was having the familiar feelings, like the ones he's

had when visiting many other locales over the past 20 years or so. This strange place where he stood on an early autumn day in 2001 was also lonely, forlorn and even a bit spooky.

Bill is a grave finder. He had come here with his friend, a Canmore history buff who spent every available weekend researching and exploring ghost towns. However, while Bill shares a similar passion for history, his travels hadn't usually taken him to ghost towns, but to lost or abandoned cemeteries and burial sites, many far removed from the perimeters of long-forgotten settlements. Bill doesn't use a shovel or ground-penetrating, radar-scanning equipment. His entire apparatus consists of two rather ordinary-looking, L-shaped welding rods, the kind that anyone can pick up at a hardware store. These he uses as divining rods. Most people refer to Bill as a diviner, or dowser.

Diviners are a shadowy clan of self-proclaimed eccentrics, usually unknown even to each other. Most of the time they hike or walk alone to remote spots to hunt for historical or natural curiosities, such as old treasures, artifacts or water—the best-known object of dowsing. Unlike most of his fellow enthusiasts, Bill is pleased to talk about his hobby, even if his blood starts to boil with contempt for conventional historians.

"I think a lot of this is just beginning to be understood by official people, official historians," says Bill. "I very much dislike a book in which 95 percent of it is footnotes. That's like, 'Look how smart I am; look what I have discovered' and 'Look where I have found it,' but there is no emotion, not a feeling for those vanished people as human beings."

Bill has been handling rods since he retired as the postmaster in Eatonia, Saskatchewan, about two decades ago. He's also been a tree surgeon and a tombstone salesman, and has written books of history, poetry and folklore—nine in all. Since turning to divining, he has dedicated his missions to finding pieces of historical puzzles that lead to further human truths about a place, a time and a passion. For Bill, those truths often start at lost or abandoned gravesites.

"In the hard-headed world of disbelievers, I refer to myself as an inexpensive, easily portable magnetometer," says Bill, whose explanations of truth and fact often resemble major proclamations from a testy town crier. "I say that the rods, held in parallel, always cross over magnetic anomalies. I use cautious words, saying that I have discovered a number of rectangular anomalies, large and small, which approximate the dimensions of human graves. I don't make an absolute claim to have found unmarked human burials, but there are no doubts in my own mind."

Back in Saskatchewan, Bill's work has taken him to distant acreages, desolate cow pastures and pioneer rural churches. He has even been called upon to walk through mud and debris in ditches alongside roads that were laid out by past government surveyors over land they didn't know was once used for burial. In 2000, for example,

Bill not only located 91 unmarked graves in the Rural Municipality of Happyland cemetery, but also discovered that three of them were now in what was a deep roadside ditch. The graveyard, he revealed, had been fenced three different times, along three different boundaries. The following year, in the nearby Rural Municipality of Newcombe, he investigated one pioneer cemetery with only five markers. When he was finished, he'd discovered an additional 49 graves—another 49 missing pieces of historical information for the municipality.

In the spring of 2002, Bill was asked by Eatonia town officials to help them find a water line behind a house where his cousin used to live. "They were having trouble and confusion with all of the water lines around there. I managed to locate them, but I also inadvertently found Bert's remarkable outhouse."

Bert was Bert Dormer, a man who Bill remembered had cheerfully supplied Eatonia with one of the town's best-ever gambling establishments, liquor joints and houses of ill repute. "I knew the history of the place. It had been referred to as the Pleasure Palace," says Bill. Bert was, by Bill's account, well liked by citizens of the community. A measure of that affection was the fact that town officials classified his home only as a residence, even though it was in the business district. Town folks refused to acknowledge any dark side to the bootlegger's colourful character.

"Bert had so many customers that he had to keep moving

his outhouse as the hole filled up," Bill explains. "Eventually he got a well driller to come and put in a 50-foot hole. That's what I found."

The God-forsaken place that Bill had found in the Alberta mountains didn't have any water lines, none that he noticed anyway. There were, however, remnants of many outhouses and cellars from years gone by, especially over a rise above the clearing. Rusted tin cans and odd-shaped bits of steel lay scattered about. This, Bill's friend told him, was once the mine site for a place called Georgetown, a ghost town since 1916.

The community was first laid out in 1910, amid great hopes and expectations for a new British-financed coal mine venture, the Georgetown Collieries (later named the Canmore Navigation Coal Company). Although not far from the town of Canmore, Georgetown's location was considered somewhat remote in its day. It was a significant undertaking for the mining company to cut a road from Canmore to the settlement over the mountain benches and through the dense alpine brush. But when some sort of order was established for the 200 or so miners and their families, Georgetown became one of the more comfortable coal-mining communities of its day. By 1913, it had at least 40 one- and two-bedroom homes overlooking an alpine meadow. Each house had running water and electricity. The town also had a general store, bunkhouse for single men and a combination one-room school and community hall. The school–community hall was also used for funerals, a

The coal-mining town of Georgetown in 1912.

point of great interest to Bill and others who have attempted to uncover more about the little-known human history of Georgetown.

Although the onset of the First World War increased demand for the mine's bituminous coal, staggering production and shipping costs soon doomed Georgetown. When mine operations closed in 1916, the town was quickly abandoned. Homes and businesses were barged down the Bow River to Canmore. Many of the miners and families followed, settling in Canmore and Bankhead to the west.

Since then, Georgetown has become nothing more than a footnote to the history of the Canmore area. The meadow under the former townsite is only a pit stop for cross-country skiers in the winter and hikers and mountain bikers in the summer. Visitors approaching the meadow from the east can see a few commemorative plaques (sadly, marred by bullet holes), but few people pause to read them. A furious summer windstorm in 1999 has left the ghost town more of a natural curiosity than a historical one.

Over 90 years since the town's establishment, there are no living survivors of the old community to offer first-hand information about the people who lived and died there. Neither is there much historical information available in archives, museums or libraries.

Edna (Hill) Appleby's 1975 book, *Canmore: The Story of an Era*, includes a few brief passages about the community, as do some academic history papers. Regional newspaper reports from 1912 to 1916 scarcely mention it, other than to say that so-and-so from Georgetown was visiting someone in Banff, Canmore or Bankhead. None of these sources mentions a cemetery. And researchers have only been able to find Georgetown death records for coal miner Andre Dolinsky (March 10, 1916), Willie Wardrop (1915) and Katie Wardrop (1916)—but there's no record of where they are buried.

At the old townsite, Bill followed his friend past the cement ruins, once the foundation of the mine manager's residence. They crawled over fallen logs and deeper into the gloom of what was left of the storm-ravaged forest. They came across one of the pieces of the gravesite puzzle that his friend had found during a previous visit. Around the base of one large tree was a tight collar of stones, slowly disappearing under a growing bulge of sod and moss. The pair found more trees with stone collars. Bill extended his divining rods and both swung dramatically, crossing each other at 90 degrees and moving slightly upward.

Bill noted that west of every tree here was a rectangular magnetic anomaly with dimensions about the size of a standard human grave. "These towering trees were once saplings planted at the foot of new graves, and whatever markers there may have been at the head of the graves have long since rotted away," he concluded.

As he continued to struggle to find a way through the thick barriers of brush and fallen trees, his divining rods registered a different rectangular pattern. His past experience told him it was the fenceline that once enclosed a cemetery plot. He thought there must be more anomalies within this perimeter, but he was starting to feel the altitude and was getting tired and cold. He took a break, but was somewhat troubled.

His thoughts went back to October 2000, when he was asked by federal government officials in Saskatchewan to examine the Frog Lake Cemetery, a national historic site maintained by Parks Canada. There, Bill discovered 12 gravelike magnetic anomalies outside the existing fences, as well as errors in the marking of burials inside the cemetery boundaries.

He recalled that he was lightly clothed and barehanded, whereas his companions were all warmly dressed. He wasn't cold, though—at least not initially—because he was concentrating on his rods, acutely aware of their slightest quiver. However, when he finished a thorough sweep of the site, he began to shake uncontrollably. "Piling on heavier clothing warmed my body, but nothing could dissolve the core of icy cold lodged inside me," he recounted. "The atmosphere of Frog Lake throbs with fear and sorrow."

At Georgetown, Bill was touched by the same cold he encountered at Frog Lake. He was moved by the same sense of gloom and despair he felt along the Saskatchewan flatlands.

"There are graves among those trees," he again declared, pausing to scan over the alpine glade. "There are people buried there who passed through all the repetitious commonalities of human existence. I felt babies, young infants who scarcely lived at all."

Bill was finished with his task. It was late afternoon and the shadows were getting longer. The sun was falling and the approaching cooler mountain air added to Bill's unsettled state. He was more subdued than when he first arrived at Georgetown. His friend did most of the talking and was anxious to hear Bill's verdict. "Would you say there is a good chance that we have found Georgetown's cemetery?" he asked Bill.

The elderly dowser paused and after careful deliberation answered tersely, "At least a fifty-fifty chance." But he went on. "It felt like the green floor was seeping into the air. I cannot really explain this. The surroundings were taking me over."

Not long after their hike to Georgetown, Bill's friend told provincial government officials about the diviner's probe. Aside from a few past archaeological and environmental studies at the site, officials had never given the Georgetown site serious thought. They were, however, intrigued with Bill's findings, though they stressed that their prime directive was not to disclose too much information to the public, as increased attention might lead to further vandalism and unwanted treasure hunting.

Two years later, Bill's Georgetown visit still brought him unsettling sensations. He conceded there may be a spirit world out there, perhaps even answering his divining probes.

Asked if he'd consider returning to visit the Georgetown site, he says, "Usually I make quick decisions, but this one I want to defer. My first visit to the place was a physical ordeal. I'm a flatlander; I need oxygen-rich prairie air. I also carry a large load of years. As the days pass, however, I'm conscious of being drawn more completely into the company of ghosts.

"Perhaps I will go to Georgetown again—and perhaps not. Today, I think I want to avoid any further contact with the presences in Georgetown's haunted forest."

Honoured Guests, Honourable Hosts

VERDA JOHNSON WAS AMAZED. A colleague at Exshaw's municipal district office, chuckling at his discovery, informed her that at least five residences on the Stoney Indian Reserve had family members with the name Verda— which was Swedish and hardly a moniker that sounded like an old-fashioned First Nations name.

"If you check one of the residence maps for the Morley reserve, you'll see that," says Verda, who was a bookkeeper at the Exshaw office from 1991 to 1998. "I don't think the people on the reserve would have thought of that name themselves unless they'd known me. They must have liked this little blonde girl enough to name their children after me."

Yes, the little blonde girl had been a big hit with the locals. She was given gifts of handmade beaded bracelets and coats, and she dressed in moccasins and Native buckskin jackets.

It was nearly half a century earlier, in 1948, when eight-year-old Verda first met the people of the Stoney Indian Reserve. Her carpenter father, Otto, came to Ozada from Winnipeg to work as a construction foreman at the new tipple. The town was created when Otto Johnson's company, the Kananaskis Exploration and Development Company (a subsidiary of Nordegg's Brazeau Collieries) leased 80 acres of land from the Stonies. The company constructed the tipple and processing plant to make briquettes from coal trucked in from the Ribbon Creek mine, located 30 kilometres south in the Kananaskis Valley.

Verda was the only child in her family of four girls and three boys to come west with her parents. Her siblings—Viola, Vilma, Vivian, Vernon, Vennard and Vidor—were older and moving on with their own lives. Vidor, or Johnny as his family often called him, came two years later to Ozada to work at the tipple and to thrill Stoney teenagers with his antique cream-coloured sports coupe. "It was a real hit. He was like a playboy," remembers Verda.

The tiny Ozada settlement was located three kilometres northeast of the present-day junction of Highway 40 and the Trans-Canada Highway. It is hidden from the highway by a low hill. Before the arrival of the tipple, Ozada was only

The decaying ruins of a 1950s automobile litter the abandoned townsite of Ozada, which closed in the early 1950s when coal-processing operations ended.

a railway whistle stop along the barren flats of the reserve. The area's previous claim to fame was the German prisoner-of-war camp located on the Morley Flats about three kilometres southwest of the townsite. The camp operated for less than a year in 1942, temporarily housing prisoners who had been captured in the Africa campaigns before they were sent to the permanent facilities in Medicine Hat and Lethbridge. It was an imposing place during its brief tenure as a prison, with 28 guard towers and a barbed-wire fence surrounding 3,400 tents and up to 13,000 prisoners of war. By 1948, the camp site resembled a ghost town, with its few remaining buildings and towers sitting empty on the windswept flats.

Life in Ozada was simple from the start, with no more than 75 people ever living there. In the beginning, homes were scarce for the residents. In their first year, Verda and her parents shared a small house with another family, with each group having only two rooms. The following summer, the Johnsons moved into a tent while Otto built the family a house. Most homes in Ozada at the time were equipped with electricity but not running water. A wood stove provided heat. Two communal water wells were constructed, one at the cookhouse and another at the west end of the townsite. Under most kitchen sinks was a slop pail; behind most homes was an outhouse.

Verda quickly discovered that she was the only white child in the new settlement. None of the other miners' children had yet arrived. However, men from the Stoney Indian Reserve were also hustling for jobs at the plant and when they were hired they brought their wives and children to live just outside Ozada. To Verda's delight, some of the children were her own age. Before long, the diminutive blonde girl had found a friend, a Stoney girl named Mina.

Mina's father worked at the tipple, and her family lived in a tent at the west end of the townsite. Mina quickly introduced Verda to the most popular recreational activity along the flats: riding horses—bareback or with a saddle.

"I rode the horses that belonged to the Natives. They were all over the place, roaming freely. The Stonies would go out on the flats between Ozada and Seebe in the spring and catch the ones they wanted to ride that summer," says Verda. "Horses were part of their wealth. All Stonies had horses and saddles."

Mixing with the Stonies became a natural way of life for Ozada residents. Verda and the other white children who gradually arrived spent most of their days with them, playing or at school in Seebe and later Exshaw.

"The Stonies had this mysticism, and a lot of superstitions. I can remember Mina's grandmother telling me about her dreams and what would happen," says Verda. "Some of them were kind of frightening."

More often than not for the past 300 years, the dreams of the Stonies turned to heartbreak and tragedy along the eastern slopes of the Canadian Rockies. It's believed they first established themselves in Alberta in the 17th century, following a series of devastating smallpox outbreaks in their native American territory. The Stonies, known then as the Assiniboine, had split with the mighty Sioux a century earlier when they lived near the headwaters of the Mississippi River.

"You can call us Mountain Assiniboines, or Rocky Mountain Sioux," said the late George McLean, Chief Walking Buffalo, the beloved patriarch and elder statesman of the Stonies. "How did we happen to settle up against the mountains? Well, it was smallpox that drove us to these parts."

Always nomadic by nature, the fractured group, then allied with the Crees, began a long northwestern migration that took them first to the Lake Winnipeg region and then westward through the Saskatchewan River system. By the 18th century, there were scattered bands of Stonies and Crees hunting all along the eastern slopes of the Rocky Mountains.

The Alberta Stonies separated into several small bands in the 19th century, including the semi-plains Bearspaw along the foothills and south to the Crowsnest Pass, the Chiniki in the Bow River region, and the Goodstoney, a woodland people near the Kootenay Plains and the North Saskatchewan River. These bands, adopting many of the customs of their plains cousins, frequently camped together and hunted elk, deer and moose in the mountains and foothills.

In 1873, Methodist missionaries George and John McDougall moved into what is now the town of Morley to establish a permanent mission. They had visions of introducing the three Stoney tribes to an agricultural way of life. Four years later, the federal government, in a bid to consolidate the Stonies in the Morley area, asked them to sign Treaty 7, although it disenfranchised some band members from their traditional Kootenay Plains and Bighorn lands. Meanwhile, as it became obvious the Morley flats were not suited for agriculture, the Stonies continued their tradition of hunting. Over the next 75 years, the Stonies were to endure famine, poverty, chronic unemployment and other serious health and social problems.

The white Ozada residents were aware of the plight of Stonies in the late 1940s and 1950s. But they also knew them as kind, generous and spiritual people who were always true to their word. Too often, however, white interests at every government and business level seemed to be trying to squeeze out the Stoney's culture and dignity.

"One thing that I remember vividly was when kids were taken away from their families and sent to the residential schools. It was in vogue then at Morley," said Bryan Fleming, a former resident at Ozada. "There was a dormitory where they kept the school-aged children. The parents were very much against the school because they didn't get to know their kids. The children went home at Christmas, Easter and during the summer holidays, but otherwise the idea was to indoctrinate them into the white man's way. There was nothing the Stonies could do about it, and it caused a lot of sadness and anger."

Bryan moved to Ozada in 1949 when he was five. His father, Vince, was the weigh-scale operator at the briquette plant and custodian of the entire Ozada site until he passed away in 1967. Over the years, Vince became good friends with many Stonies, including Tom Kaquitts, Nelson Rabbit, Ken Soldier, Frank Powderface, Nat Hunter, Tom LaBelle and, of course, George McLean, or Walking Buffalo. "We knew him as the medicine man," says Bryan. Walking Buffalo was also renowned, even in 1950 when he was getting on in years, for being one of the reserve's better riders. The first time he'd been on a horse was as an infant in a cradle-pouch with his grandmother.

Being white and only a young boy, Bryan faced the same problems as Verda had in finding someone to play with. But as he got little older, he too discovered that horses were a convenient icebreaker and good way to make friends.

"Nelson Rabbit and Ken Soldier sold my dad on the idea of getting horses. We paid $50 for an okay horse and $100 for a good horse. They weren't quarter horses or anything like that. They were multi-breeds with excellent stamina and could keep going forever," says Bryan.

He regularly saddled up and rode across the flats to meet his native pals. Sometimes they went to Bow Fort or to Chiniki Lake to camp, fish or swim. He was even invited to visit secret burial grounds.

Bryan became accustomed to the fact that the Stonies didn't have much in the way of possessions, but their kindness and hospitality always made up for whatever material shortages were apparent. He remembers one Christmas

Eve being invited into the home of Moses Ear, the reserve policeman, and seeing first-hand the effort some Stonies made to create a traditional holiday and impress others. "They had a Christmas tree up with candles on it. It was interesting to see, but also looked fairly dangerous," he says.

As the Stonies began to know and trust their white neighbours in Ozada, they honoured them with invitations to the Sun Dance, an ancient three-day event of fasting, dancing and praying to celebrate young men becoming braves and entering manhood. Invitations to the event on the reserve were extended only to non-Stonies who were liked and trusted.

Verda was still a child when she went to her first Sun Dance, but remembers well the elaborate and colourful ceremony. There was a tall, stout pole in the centre of a lodge, rising upward through the ceiling. This was the Tree of Life, and bright silk cloth adorned its branches both inside and outside the lodge. Verda was wide-eyed as she watched the native dancers move day and night inside the enclosed structure to the beat of a tribal tom-tom drummer, circling the Tree of Life. Among their many prayers, the young men asked the Great Spirit for guidance in all decisions affecting their people and the uncertain future ahead.

While the Stonies prayed for a better future for themselves, the clock was running out for Ozada. When Ribbon Creek ceased operations in February 1952, it was also the end for the Ozada processing plant. Rising freight rates to eastern Canada and the expense of transporting coal from Ribbon Creek no longer made either venture viable. It was the only time that two ghost towns were created in the Canadian Rockies by the same stroke of a company pen.

Verda's family went back and forth between the two townsites until 1955, when they moved to Canmore. Vince Fleming was asked by the company to stay and look after the Ozada townsite and its abandoned buildings and equipment. By 1954, the Flemings were the last family left. Bryan stayed until 1964 and then left for university.

Today, Bryan still occasionally visits Ozada. He's never forgotten the pleasures of the simple and wondrous life he had living in Stoney country. "It was a place that few white people really had access to," says Bryan. "I wouldn't have traded growing up there for being anywhere else."

Not for the Weak of Heart

NO MATTER WHAT WEATHER OR what terrain Norman Holt had to face, he always pushed on fearlessly. And while his contemporaries in 1950 might have considered his life on the road to be as wild and dangerous as it got, he loved it.

Norman, who became a long-distance truck driver in 1932, savoured challenging and spine-tingling hauls. There was nothing more relaxing for him than to drive a big truck and trailer through a route that would make lesser men shake and sweat, if they didn't bail out altogether.

"I was just a hick in the sticks, but I had a lot of guts," says Norman, who came from the small Central Alberta community of Bashaw. Norman was also a champion long-distance runner, and from 1932 to 1964 he held the Alberta record for the fastest half mile.

His wife, Jeanette, was a superb athlete as well, an exceptional fastball player whose skills were coveted south of the border. During the Second World War, she was invited to play for the Chicago Wrigleys in the upstart national women's league. She declined, though, and at about the same time Norman put the brakes on running. The two were about to take on a different challenge.

In 1949, a new coal mine was opening up in Alberta's mountainous and much-storied Kananaskis Valley. This area was the traditional home of the nomadic Stoney people, a mountain Sioux band. British explorer John Palliser led the first celebrated expedition through the Kananaskis Pass in 1857 to investigate the existence of rumoured resources, including gold and silver, in the remote mountain ranges. Along the way, expedition member Dr. James Hector made the first geological study of the region, partly in response to the gold fever that was spreading like an alpine wildfire through central BC.

Subsequent prospectors followed Hector's lead to look for gold in the Kananaskis, but none succeeded. Legend has it that one pair, Lemon and Blackjack, did find a huge seam in 1870, but the two apparently argued over whether to begin digging immediately or to return later to stake the claim. Their bickering ended, so the story goes, when Lemon murdered Blackjack with a camp axe while he slept. Half-crazed by what he'd done, Lemon reportedly paced "like a caged wild beast" around a campfire the entire night with a gun under his arm, his soul torn apart by guilt and remorse. When daylight broke, he mounted his horse and rode back to Tobacco Plains, Montana, where the prospecting party had started its ill-fated quest.

Where gold failed to give people the wealth they were after in the Kananaskis, coal was at least making some headway. The new mine in Norman's future was located at an isolated locale called Ribbon Creek, situated halfway up Mount Allan. The only traffic there was created by migrating elk and moose. Even the townsite's name was not for certain. It was known by some map-makers as Ribbon Creek, but few people ever called the community that. The *Gazetteer of Canada* listed it as the Locality of Kovach, after district ranger Joe Kovach, but that name too was rarely used. Most folks just referred to the place as "Ribbon Crick" or "The Camp."

For more than four decades, the coalfields at Ribbon Creek had been coveted but never developed. They were first staked in 1907 by Martin Nordegg. Nordegg went on to develop the famous coalfields of Big West Country and to build the town that had his name. By 1948, Nordegg had long been eased out of his western Canadian coalfield operations, but Brazeau Collieries was anxious to get its Kananaskis coalfields in production. The company was eager to capitalize on opportunities in the

Ontario anthracite coal market and the popularity of fuel briquettes, already a successful venture at Nordegg.

However, there was one major problem in the Kananaskis for Brazeau Collieries. There was no railroad into the mountainous valley and no immediate way to get the coal out.

Enter Norman. He was making a name for himself in the Alberta trucking industry, and Brazeau turned to him. In 1949, he secured the trucking contract to haul coal out and deliver it 30 kilometres north to the company's tipple and processing plant at Ozada, a railway siding on the Stoney Indian Reserve. From there, it was full speed ahead to the rich Ontario markets.

When Ribbon Creek was up and running, with Norman's convoy of trucks delivering coal non-stop to Ozada, it was one of the most unique and challenging coal-mining operations in the Canadian Rockies. Norman hired 40 drivers to haul the coal on the winding, switchbacked, gravel and dirt road from Ribbon Creek to the flats of Ozada. The route was not for the weak of heart.

Work was done in two shifts, one beginning at 8 a.m. and the other at 4 p.m. Twenty-one trucks, equipped with seven-metre trailers, each hauled 24 tonnes of coal on a run. Norman paid his drivers 25 percent on whatever he got for a load. So, if a truck brought in $200 a day, the driver got $50, which was great money at the time.

One of the most challenging sections of the road was over Barrier Hill, where many motor vehicles couldn't negotiate the steep incline, especially in icy winter conditions. "With the first storm in the mountains, we were shut down for a day and a half. When we were able to get going again, we lost five trucks in one day," says Norman. "The drivers ditched them because they weren't used to the mountain driving. The insurance company wanted to pull out right away," he adds with a laugh.

Norman's bills added up. His tire costs were never under $3,500 a month, and that was when tires were going for $60 each, not about $450 like they do today. He switched to heavy trucks in 1951 and purchased a whole new fleet, each with an extra transmission for the needed boost over the mountain terrain. Norman's equipment payments were $10,000 a month, a huge sum in that day. But he had few complaints about his drivers, some of whom used unique ways to get over the dreaded Barrier Hill.

"One chap named Shoemaker had a three-ton Ford truck, and if he had a few extra pounds over his normal load, he could not make the hill," says Norman. "The steepest part was at the very last. He'd get just about to the top and the motor would kick out. When that happened, he'd back down and then make his dog—which he always had with him—get out of the truck. The dog would run alongside as Shoemaker headed back up the hill. He'd always make the grade that way, time after time."

The men Norman hired came from all parts of Alberta and beyond. With jobs booming after the Second World War, it

A snowstorm blankets the town of Ribbon Creek in 1950. The town, also known as Kovach, was abandoned in 1952 when coal-mining operations ended. The remains of Ribbon Creek, deep in the Kananaskis Valley of the Canadian Rockies, were left undisturbed until finally bulldozed in 1969.

wasn't the easiest sales pitch to convince drivers, especially single men, to come to the Kananaskis wilderness. There weren't many amenities in Ribbon Creek for anybody.

At first, single men had to stay in bunkhouses, which could accommodate up to 100. In later years, the workers were able to buy three-room houses for $1,200 from the mining company. Lack of food in the town was another problem. For the first while, villagers drove to Canmore, Banff or Seebe to get their groceries. In 1950, however, an arrangement was made with the Seebe General Store owner, Ken Lyster, to bring in groceries once a week to residents. Also lacking was a hotel or bar. Although Lil and Harold Falt operated a café for a time, it burned down and was never rebuilt. Fortunately for the men, they were still able to get their meals at a large log cookhouse where Scotty and Nellie Patterson were the chefs.

Perhaps one of the biggest problems for the single men, however, was the lack of female companionship. For at least the first two years of Ribbon Creek's brief lifespan, there were no single women in the community. On their days off, the men headed to either Canmore or Cochrane for some good times, though sometimes they wished they'd stayed at home.

"One night, three of the boys took the ambulance out. I didn't know it," says Norman, "but they had their freedom and went to Canmore. There were two girls walking down the street and of course the boys pulled up alongside, talked to them for awhile, and made a date. The girls gave them the address of their house and told them to come down in about a half an hour and knock on the door. They did—and two husbands came out. That taught those boys a lesson."

In 1950, the single men got a boost when the community's first schoolteacher arrived, a beautiful 21-year-old woman named Isabel Shanks. That she was the daughter of mine manager David Shanks put her, unfortunately, somewhat out of reach of most would-be suitors.

When Isabel arrived in late August of that year, she was paralyzed with fear—not because she had to deal with 100 or so lovestruck and lonely single men, but because Ribbon Creek was her first teaching job. This was also the first time children in Ribbon Creek wouldn't have to travel 32 kilometres to Seebe for their classes. A one-room school was built that year, and Isabel, a recent graduate from the University of Alberta, was hired.

It was not an easy task, even for a veteran teacher. Isabel had more than 20 students in Grades 1 to 8, and most of them were just as apprehensive as she was. In addition to preparing lessons for eight different grades, the young teacher had to shift around from one group of students to another all day long. Carol D'Amico was one of Isabel's students, a bright seven-year-old in Grade 2. Isabel found a special task for Carol as her unofficial assistant, helping other students in her own grade and beyond.

"I thought she was wonderful, probably because I was the teacher's pet," says Carol. "There was an old wood stove in the school and I was happy to stoke it and to be the one to clean the blackboard—all those little teacher's pet things."

Isabel's popularity didn't end with the single men and her students. She was also loved by the DPs, or displaced persons. They were the European men who came to the Kananaskis looking for a better way of life after the Second World War. Many had been prisoners of war at the Kananaskis Camp near what is now Barrier Lake. A group of them asked Isabel to teach them English. They were living in the bunkhouse with the Canadian men and having problems understanding certain expressions. Isabel agreed and at least one evening a week she met with them to discuss the finer points of the English language.

"One man, I remember, went up to the blackboard and copied out an expression he needed help understanding. I had to laugh," says Isabel. "It was 'sonofabitch.' I guess he'd heard it in the bunkhouse or read it in one of the western stories the men liked to read."

Isabel left Ribbon Creek at the end of the first school year, in 1951. Her father was transferred back to Nordegg, and she found another teaching job outside the valley.

That year, rail freight rates to Ontario markets increased. The company also discovered it was difficult to sell its Ozada briquettes. When Brazeau Collieries shut down its Ribbon Creek mine early the next year, it was the permanent end to all Kananaskis coal mining. Miners quickly packed up their families and belongings and headed to other coal towns. Ribbon Creek lingered as a wilderness ghost town for many years. The final demolition of its buildings occurred in 1969.

The closing of the mine left Norman in financial ruins. The mine owed him money and never paid it. Promises were made about the mine soon reopening, but that never happened. Norman and his family left Ribbon Creek in the fall of 1952. The mine closure cost him all his trucks two years later and left him tens of thousands of dollars in debt. However, he refused to declare bankruptcy. Instead, he negotiated with his creditors to pay off his entire debt in 11 years. Returning to Bashaw, he resumed his trucking business. At the age of 89 and with more than 5 million kilometres under his belt, Norman was still trucking. He has no regrets.

"People used to say to me that Ribbon Creek took 11 years off my life while I cleared my debt," says Norman, "but I'd say, 'No, it didn't. It added 11 years to my life.' It was all new to us, working and living in the mountains. I still think it was the best job we were ever on."

CROWSNEST

Borderline Capers

WHEN GUESTS OF THE Inn on the Border call for room service, they have to dial long distance. The phone is in BC and their food is in Alberta. And 18-year-olds wanting a beer after a day of snowmobiling have to stick to the east side of the bed and breakfast. It's in Alberta, where that province's liquor laws prevail. The west side of the bed and breakfast is in BC, where the legal drinking age is 19.

The inn proprietors chuckle over the oddities of their operation—the result of their building sitting smack on the border and spilling over on either side—though it's not always a laughing matter when government bureaucrats get involved. Owner Tammy Tracey can talk the day away with stories about star-crossed government bill payments or what provincial agency is in charge when the lights go out.

The Inn on the Border is one of the last historic landmarks still standing in Crowsnest, a tiny hamlet that sits on the boundary between Alberta and BC. The townsite is at the end of a service road, just off the fabulously scenic Highway 3 through the Crowsnest Pass. The mountainous wilderness surrounding Crowsnest is unquestionably beautiful, but living in the border town comes with a price—and no one knows that more than Tammy and her husband, Darren. That price is regular bureaucratic wrangling.

The Traceys are considered to be Alberta residents, but they pay BC business taxes and their property taxes go to the District of Sparwood in BC. When the power goes off, they call BC Hydro first and then TransAlta, because the area's transformer is in Alberta. After a fire on their property a few years ago, the incident report was sent to an Alberta insurance agency by a BC fire inspector.

"We didn't expect all these problems," confesses Tammy, "because the business, not to mention the building, has been here for years."

The paperwork can be especially trying. Take the never-ending Workers' Compensation Board paperwork that went on for six years after one of Tammy's staff got hurt. The girl mistakenly told the hospital she had WCB coverage in BC. Tammy, however, was already paying for Alberta WCB coverage, as all her employees were from that province.

The issue should have ended there, but instead it triggered a maddening cross-border dispute. BC officials said Tammy owed them money. "Wrong," she told them.

After numerous letters were exchanged, Tammy was finally asked to calculate how much time her employees spent in each province when they were on the job. "I said to the guy on the phone, 'Do you think I'm going to follow my staff around all day? You must be crazy. I'm not paying into both plans. I'm writing one cheque: you people decide who I'm to pay and that's it.'" The dispute finally ended in 2002 when WCB in BC agreed that Tammy only had to pay premiums if her employees lived in that province.

Tammy's family bought the inn in 1990. It was the former Summit Hotel, one of the last buildings from Crowsnest's early pioneer days when the hamlet was home to about 700 residents. Today, Crowsnest is a ghost town, a place where all the phantoms of its past are free to walk, drink or hurt themselves on whichever side of the border they want.

For almost 100 years, the old hotel has straddled the provincial boundary. The building also sits directly on the Continental Divide. It's from up here that water sources originate and then flow either east to Hudson Bay or west to the Pacific Ocean. "We don't have to worry about anyone peeing in our water supply," says Diane Florence, Tammy's mother.

In Crowsnest's early years, it was possible to stand on

the hotel's front porch and watch some channels from the property's creek flow into Alberta and some flow into BC. That creek, known as either Andy Good Creek or Summit Creek, has also been the focus of an often bizarre boundary dispute since the 19th century. In 1898, BC coal entrepreneurs, anxious to develop a huge claim that cut across the recognized border of the time, reportedly considered altering the provincial boundary by diverting creek waters into their province. When federal government officials learned of the plan almost three decades later, they confirmed that the creek had been diverted, but not in the way they first thought. A main channel flowed into Alberta's Island Lake, while an artificial creek fed into BC's Summit Lake. The land in between—a triangular two-acre parcel of property— ended up lying, strategically, right on what was believed to be the border.

The mysterious creek diversion was traced back to Andy Good, the original owner of the Summit Hotel. Andy first arrived at this boundary location with his wife, Kate, in either 1897 or 1898. At the time, it was a railway construction site known as Bull Head, a point on the boundary of BC and what was still known then as the North-West Territories, later becoming Alberta in 1905. In 1900, a post office was opened at the site, which came to be known as Crow's Nest. The name was two words until 1930, when federal postal officials changed it to Crowsnest.

Andy and Kate started their new life with a tent-hotel,

A provincial boundary marker at Crowsnest marks the divide
between Alberta and British Columbia. The boundary runs
through the pioneer Summit Hotel, seen in the background.

constructed with slab sides and a wooden floor. The make-shift bar was replaced by a log house and later by construction of the first Summit Hotel in 1899. The two-storey hotel and bar became the toast of the Pass, a popular resort stop for tourists. It also featured wild meat supplied by French hunter Baptiste La More and, for a while, boasted the largest covered dance pavilion in BC. Andy's hotel was even renowned with hunters and outdoorsmen from the United States. An added attraction was his "zoo."

"Andy kept wild animals in cages at the back: wolves, a mountain lion, and a bear on a chain. Also a mean monkey chained in the room off the bar where Andy kept his safe," reported a former hotel guest who worked as a railway fireman in Crowsnest in 1912. "I remember one night in the bar I had the gloves on with a switchman. It was payday and he was teasing me. I boxed him until I got him close to the door of that little room. He backed up a bit into the room. The monkey took him by the seat of his pants, and he jumped up three feet at least. He didn't sit down for several days, and he never bothered me again."

It was not just chance that Andy's hotel straddled the provincial boundary so precisely, with one part of the bar in BC and the other in Alberta. Andy wanted the best of both worlds when it came to satisfying liquor laws. He figured that if the laws changed in either province at any time, he'd be ready to move his patrons around the bar accordingly.

But Andy's caper didn't last. A few years after his creek

diversion, federal government officials in Alberta and BC started haggling over the administration of the natural resources on both sides of the border. During this squabbling, Andy was forced to remove his diversion, which was promptly renamed "Andy's Dry Run." He passed away in 1916.

Jurisdiction over the triangular piece of land between the creek and Andy's diversion was never quite determined, or at least fully accepted. The Alberta and BC governments tried to settle the boundary dispute in the 1940s. Both governments agreed that a straight line should be used for the boundary instead of the meandering alpine creek, which could so easily fall victim to human alterations. Although government officials signed papers, the agreement only resulted in more questions and controversy. Following the boundary resolution negotiations of the 1940s, Ian Turner, a historian from Cranbrook, BC, took a serious interest in the debate.

"He was good friends with Shorty Ross, a former owner of the hotel. I think they'd started talking about the laws in Alberta and BC," says Diane Florence. "There was so much controversy as to where the actual border was. Ian started digging into the history, and what he discovered was that the piece had never been claimed by either province."

Ian Turner devoted many years of research to settling the issue for himself, and after a lengthy investigation, he bought the property in 1979 and pronounced it a principality, independent of either BC or Alberta. He named his new principality "Turner's Kingdom" and claimed he would convince the British monarchy to recognize his new principality as part of the Commonwealth. Turner's plan never did come about, but it's become a popular piece of Crowsnest Pass folklore.

"It was more of a joke than anything, but he was just trying to see how far he could push it," says Tammy. "He started taking it one step at a time, produced a coat of arms, and was trying to get his own currency. He attempted to register his coat of arms with the government, but he never heard back."

Tammy owns the property now, and Summit Creek is no longer the topic of a boundary debate. It flows harmlessly out of the way, east of the inn on the Alberta side and into Island Lake. Unfortunately, new boundary issues have arisen, and there's an ongoing dispute over the hotel property line.

An independent surveyor Tammy hired in 1998 told her the property line of the bible camp to the east of her land runs through the inn's kitchen, and the property line for the land south of the hotel runs through the hot tub. Adding to the confusion is the fact that this surveyor's findings contradict another set of conclusions drawn up in the 1980s by experts hired by the Canadian Pacific Railway, which owns property north and west of the inn.

"I'm thankful we have good neighbours who don't tell us to get off their land," says Tammy.

Business is good and the setting can't be beat. So, for now, Tammy has let the property-line issue go. "The paperwork remains the number 1 problem," she says, but she knows it goes with the territory—borderline territory.

Gone But Not Forgotten

BERTHA AVOLEDO'S SCHOOL DAY STARTED with brilliant sunshine and the promise of a glorious field trip. The previous evening had been windy and blustery, but today the weather was calm and blue skies prevailed.

It was late June 1929, and there were only a few days left of school before the summer break. Bertha and her Grade 3 classmates collected themselves in a frenzied, giggling group outside Maple Leaf School in Bellevue, a small town in Alberta's Crowsnest Pass area. They were joining another 100 students at the school for a rare field trip. They were hiking to Lille, a ghost town that lay about 14 kilometres northwest of Bellevue in a wilderness valley between the Livingstone and Blairmore mountain ranges. Lille had been a ghost town since 1913, when its coal mine closed.

Bertha's teacher, whom she adored, was Miss Margaret Hallworth. She came from a family of teachers. Her sister Florence also taught in Bellevue, and her late mother was the former superintendent of the local Methodist Sunday School. There was also a Lille connection in Miss Hallworth's family. Her father, Albert, was the pit boss at Bellevue's West Canadian Collieries Mine, the same company that had run the operation at Lille.

Miss Hallworth was hoping the hike to Lille would be a good history lesson for her students, even if most of them opted to daydream and chatter away during much of the outing. She had heard rumours that Lille's many abandoned buildings were about to be torn down, and she wanted the children to see the town before it was gone.

The hike to Lille was long and in some places arduous for the students. The trail skirted up behind Bellevue. The first part of the route went along a small creek, past the town cemetery, and then climbed a hill and carried on into the mountains.

Bertha and her classmates didn't know much about Lille. Their parents had perhaps mentioned it a few times, but the kids had never paid much attention. It was just another coal-mining place in the Crowsnest Pass where people once worked and lived. Some of the children, however, had heard bits and pieces about murders and other intriguing stories related to the old town.

The crumbling ruins of Lille's No. 1 coal mine power house in the Crowsnest Pass. The mine and town closed in 1913.

As her charges trekked along the path, Miss Hallworth realized her hands were full. Children who were mere days away from a summer holiday were not the most attentive students. Nevertheless, she stopped her group every few hundred metres or so to point out a patch of colourful wild-flowers, examine peculiar rock formations or speculate about odd pieces of old metal. She used the latter rusty relics as props to tell her students about Lille's brief history.

Coal had first been prospected there in 1901 by Jules-Justin Fleutot and Charles Remy, two geologists and entre-preneurs who represented BC Gold Fields Ltd. The first year at the site was difficult, as supplies could only be packed in with horses. A wagon trail was built the following year. It made deliveries easier, but Fleutot and Remy knew a rail line was the best answer. However, the pair needed money to build a railroad, and that sort of funding was only avail-able outside Canada.

After some effort, Fleutot secured funding from a Belgian and French consortium for the wilderness mine site, briefly called French Camp. A new company, West Canadian Collieries Ltd., was formed in 1903. Many of the consortium partners were from the town of Lille in northern France, and it became the name of the new Canadian coal mine. The investment gave Lille the new railroad—the Frank and Grassy Mountain Railway—it badly needed. The line was a true engineering wonder of its day: an 11-kilometre spur line that linked Frank (the closest established community to the south) to Lille. It snaked and climbed 239 metres up the valley of Gold Creek, along hair-raising switchbacks. After crossing 23 timber trestles, the trains entered Lille at the junction of Gold and Morin creeks.

As Bertha and her classmates finally neared Lille, the first buildings came into view along a flat meadow, with Grassy Mountain looming high behind the townsite. All chatter stopped. It suddenly seemed odd that there was no one to greet them. Even though most of the buildings were standing, the town was completely empty—left, it seemed, exactly the way it was the moment the mine closed in 1913.

The students began to scan the empty structures before them, picking out the most interesting ones to explore. Despite the abandonment, almost every building looked like it must have when the town closed. Time and the elements had clearly left their mark, but there was very little other damage or vandalism. In fact, each structure seemed to cling to the here and now, seeming taller and nobler in spite of the emptiness and sorrow of human neglect.

Bertha had never before entered a ghost town, or felt the sensation of a failed community. "It was eerie," she says now in remembrance. "It was strange to think that people had once been there. I thought I should hear the voices of children, that there should be something there. It was so very quiet."

Dominating the haunting impression was the huge array of coke ovens poised across the town's main street, Grassy Mountain Avenue, and extending past the hotel. As Miss

Hallworth told her students, these 50 remarkable Belgian "Bernard" coking ovens had been prefabricated in Europe in 1903, with each brick numbered for easy reassembly in Lille. The Bernard coke ovens were considered at the time to be the most advanced in North America.

Early on, the community's population swelled to more than 500 as Lille rapidly developed into a fully serviced townsite. It even had a 15-bed hospital.

Miss Hallworth pointed to the remains of the magnificent two-storey Lille Hotel, at the time thought to be one of the finest in the Crowsnest Pass. Constructed by businessman Clovis Faure in 1903, the 30-room hotel was famous for its lavish interior and the elaborate terrace stretched across the front. The 540-square-metre facility, which became Lille's social centre, had a U-shaped floor plan on both floors. An exact replica was built in Bellevue shortly after Faure constructed his dream hotel in Lille. During the huge forest fire of 1910, which surrounded Lille on three sides, Faure nearly lost the hotel. Luckily, the blaze burned itself out just outside the townsite, but not before Lille had its first heroine.

Jeanie Pinkney, Miss Hallworth told her students, was the wife of Frederick Matthew Pinkney, who owned Lille's only general store with his nephew, Frederick Matthew Thompson. Jeanie was a woman of abundant energy and courage, diminutive in stature but very feisty. As the forest fire raced towards Lille, the men doused all the buildings with water while the women dug holes to bury family valuables. Women with children were becoming frantic as smoke engulfed the town and the fire approached. Jeanie, however, kept her cool. She quickly hitched horses to a wagon and drove back and forth to Frank several times, evacuating scores of women and children. In the eleventh hour, the wind changed direction and the fire ended its advance on Lille.

If Lille had its heroines, it had its villains too. According to Miss Hallworth, the story began with three Italian miners, including two brothers, who lived together and worked as a team in the mine. The brothers were contract miners, earning a healthy wage of between $10 and $20 a day. This hit a nerve with the third Italian miner who was only pulling in $2.75 daily, even though he worked longer and harder. The big difference in pay eventually led to a violent argument during a shift, a volatile dispute that continued afterwards. When the trio got home, the low-paid man immediately went upstairs for his shotgun to settle the issue. He shot one brother, who died instantly. The other ran out of the house, but the crazed man loaded up and shot him in the back. That brother died within a week.

After the shootings, the killer walked all the way to Frank and gave himself up to police. He was later sentenced to seven years in jail.

On that fine June day of 1929, it wasn't long before the students' attention shifted away from the dark tale. They began walking across town to the Lille school, which had once served about 30 students each year during the town's nine-year lifespan. The little building sat isolated and forlorn at the north end of the townsite, between the miners' residences and the more opulent homes of management officials.

Miss Hallworth took Bertha and a small group of students towards the school, reminding them to leave everything inside the way they found it. The front door opened easily to reveal student desks arranged just like they'd been left on the last day of school 16 years earlier. The teacher's desk was still at the head of the class. A few textbooks lay scattered about, and pieces of chalk rested on the blackboard ledge. Bertha picked up a piece and then hesitated. A sense of sorrow overwhelmed her. "Because it did not belong to us, I wondered if it was really right that I should be disturbing it. I felt as though I was taking something that belonged to somebody else, and it really impressed me in that way," says Bertha. "I just couldn't get over the fact that there were no children there anymore. It seemed like such a waste."

Bertha wrote her name on the chalkboard and then stopped. There wasn't anything more to say, she knew. But there and then, even at the tender age of eight, she made an important decision. Her trip to Lille—and particularly her visit with the phantom students—had left quite an impression. Bertha became a teacher and taught her first class in 1940.

Guardians of the Ghosts

IN 1979, A HALF CENTURY after Bertha Avoledo's memorable hike to Lille, long-time Crowsnest Pass resident Mary Drain received an unexpected phone call from a local oilman. He told her that a Calgary lady named Eva, who was raised and schooled in Lille, wanted to take her three sisters and brother up to the ghost town.

However, all of them were elderly and hadn't been back to Lille since the mine closed in 1913. The five siblings made a promise to their late mother that they would some day return to Lille to retrieve a forgotten copper kettle in the basement of their pioneer home.

Mary had lived in the Crowsnest Pass all her life, but had never been to Lille. That summer she took the five siblings up to the townsite. When they arrived, their former home was no longer there, just a foundation hole and a few piles of soil and decaying timber. In fact, almost everything had vanished from Lille. All that really remained were the crumbling coke ovens and two fire hydrants on the bare townsite meadow.

Their mother's kettle was nowhere to be found, but later, near the coke ovens, they discovered a porcelain door knob poking out of the ground. "They were excited with that, but felt so bad that they didn't find anything else," says Mary.

It was the family's simple reward for trying to keep a promise to their mother. However, their disappointment also underscored the longstanding frustration felt by heritage preservationists in the Crowsnest Pass and throughout the Canadian Rocky Mountains. Year after year, many of them claim, pioneer mountain history fades one step closer to oblivion.

Almost 25 years after Eva and her siblings visited Lille, there is even less to see and nobody left to offer first-hand stories about this remarkable town. Eva and the others are now deceased. The last known Lille resident reportedly died in 2002. Although the Lille site was declared a provincial historical site in 1978, scavengers have long pillaged countless bricks from the coke ovens, taking them home to construct fireplaces or driveways. Lille is close to being erased from history, and the same holds true for many other ghost towns in the Bow Valley, Big West Country and the Coal Branch.

The old lamphouse at Bankhead. Miners would pick up their lamps here before going underground.

Nevertheless, historians and preservationists in the Canadian Rockies hold a distinct advantage over their American counterparts. Most ghost towns in the American Rockies had their heyday in the mid- to late 19th century, which has now made it impossible to gather first-hand pioneer stories and much harder to recover what has already been lost or taken. Because most ghost towns in the Canadian Rockies reached their greatest prosperity in the first half of the 20th century, many pioneer residents are still alive, and at least some of the communities continue to hold significant historical artifacts worthy of preservation. But time is running out.

Heritage preservationists in the Canadian Rockies, and notably those at the grassroots community level, are fighting back, even with little government or business support. They've become the guardians of the ghosts.

Sometimes their efforts are just simple recollections passed on from one generation to another. Others contribute with literary works or art. For several years, Banff's Louis Trono delighted local residents with his weekly newspaper columns about his days growing up in Bankhead, a national park ghost town northeast of Banff that closed down in 1922. Canmore's Michael Vincent earns rave reviews for his breathtaking heritage artwork that depicts the resort town's simple but nearly forgotten pioneer mining days.

Former residents from several pioneer communities have rallied over the past decade to publish comprehensive community books, complete with histories and personal stories. Almost a half century after Mountain Park closed in the Coal Branch in 1950, former residents published the 800-page *Mountain Park Memories*. In 2002, Lucien Villeneuve, a past resident of Coal Valley, produced a photo album for his former neighbours, again nearly 50 years after the town's closure.

A similar project is underway in Rocky Mountain House to cover Big West Country. In 2000, locals in the Crowsnest Pass completed the third volume of their community's retrospective, *Crowsnest and Its People*.

Grassroots preservationists have also had modest

success in restoring pioneer cemeteries, buildings and mine workings. By far the most promising success story is in Nordegg, where the mine site received federal national historic status in 2002. A group of former Nordegg residents decided in the early 1980s that they couldn't watch their town disappear, or see the mine site possibly being turned into a cement plant. They formed the Nordegg Historical Society. Anne Belliveau-McMullen, a former resident and retired Calgary schoolteacher, decided to join the group. "I wanted to save what was left of our history," said Anne, who became the society's historian and publicist. Along the way, she also wrote a highly acclaimed book, *Small Moments in Time: The Story of Alberta's Big West Country*.

Over the past 15 years, the society has saved the mine site from the wrecker's ball, earned it provincial and national historic designation and raised hundreds of thousands of dollars for restoration.

West of the border, preservationists in BC's Crowsnest Pass have struggled long and hard to save the region's coal-mining history. The communities of Michel and Natal have vanished.

In September 1997, I was driving through the BC side of the Crowsnest Pass and stopped at Michel. It was my first time there, and I had turned off the highway to rest behind an old brick building, obviously vacant or abandoned. After a short walk to take a few landscape photographs, I was heading back to my car when I saw a bulldozer move toward the brick building. It began knocking down walls. Worried that I might get stuck behind the bulldozer's work, I quickly drove off.

I later learned that the doomed structure was a colliery building and one of Michel's last pioneer mine structures. Besides the bulldozer driver, I was the last one to see it standing. There was no one to watch it go under, no one there to honour and reflect on its noble past in this once busy valley. I felt sad for the building, wondering what human lives, dramas and adventures it had hosted. I hadn't taken any pictures of the structure and that was a mistake. Since then, I've made it my personal mission to take thousands.

The following month, I interviewed John Pearson in Banff about the forgotten grave in Anthracite. I've collected hundreds of stories since and know there are more to hear, more to record and more to preserve. Doing all that is my promise.

Bibliography

Basque, Garnet, ed. *Lost Bonanzas of Western Canada.*
Langley: Sunfire Publications Ltd., 1983.

Belliveau, Anne (McMullen). *Small Moments in Time: The Story of Alberta's Big West Country.* Calgary: Detselig Enterprises Ltd., 1999.

Clipperton, Jack. *Beautiful Banff Tour—C9.* Banff: Brewster, 1997.

Davies, Bill. *Underground at Mountain Park: A History of Coal Mining Fifty Eight Hundred Feet Above Sea Level.* Edmonton: Saka Inc., 2001.

Drain, Valerie. *Images of Lille.* Frank: Alberta Community Development/Frank Slide Interpretive Centre, 1988.

Fryer, Harold. *Ghost Towns of Alberta.* Langley: Stagecoach Publishing Company Limited/Mr. Paperback, 1976.

Kinnear, John. *Could It Happen Again.* Fernie: Fernie Free Press, 1995.

Kyba, Daniel and Jane Ross. *Exploring the Historic Coal Branch: A Guide to Jasper's Front Ranges.* Calgary: Rocky Mountain Books, 2001.

MacEwan, Grant. *Tatanga Mani, Walking Buffalo of the Stonies.* Edmonton: M.G. Hurtig, 1969.

Norton, Wayne and Naomi Miller, eds. *The Forgotten Side of the Border: British Columbia's Elk Valley and Crowsnest Pass.* Kamloops: Plateau Press, 1998.

Oltmann, Ruth. *The Valley of Rumours ... the Kananaskis.* Exshaw: Ribbon Creek Publishing Company, 1976.

Oltmann, Ruth. *My Valley ... the Kananaskis.* Calgary: Rocky Mountain Books, 1997.

Ross, Jane and William Tracy. *Hiking the Historic Crowsnest Pass.* Calgary: Rocky Mountain Books, 1992.

Ross, Toni. *Oh! The Coal Branch*. Edmonton: Mrs. Toni Ross, 1974.

Salzsauler, Mary (Lee) and Joan P. Talbot Wegert, eds. *Mountain Park Memories*. Edmonton: Try Gra-Fix Ltd., 1999.

Tingley, K.W. *For King and Country*. Edmonton: Provincial Museum of Alberta/Reidmore Books, 1995.

Turner, Ian. G. *The Crowsnest Boundary Bungle*. Cranbrook, Ian Turner, 1979.

Wardill, William. *A Gold Cuff Link and a Red Dress*. Eatonia: Speargrass Specialties, 1997.

Zeman, Gary. *Alberta on Ice*. Edmonton: Westweb Press, 1985.

Index

Acknowledgements

It would be impossible to express enough gratitude to the more than 100 people who graciously helped with this project. Sadly, it's also impossible to list everyone, and for that I apologize.

Almost without exception, every person and organization I contacted gave generously in terms of time and content. As always, there was Nordegg's Anne Belliveau-McMullen, who over the years has provided me with unlimited resources and time. Anne, who herself is a successful writer, is a stickler for facts and accuracy. Anne has become not only one of my most valuable resources over the years, but a wonderful friend to both my wife and me.

From the Coal Branch to the Crowsnest Pass, I received almost unconditional support and cooperation. Special thanks to Wendy Zack, operations manager at the Crowsnest Museum, for her hard work in supplying me with copious amounts of historical material; Eva and David Welsh, tireless volunteers for the Crowsnest Historical Society; John Kinnear, vice-president of the Fernie and District Historical Society; my employer, Red Deer Publishing; and Lucien Villeneuve, a former Coal Valley resident, who organized an amazing afternoon get-together in his Edmonton home of almost a dozen former pioneer neighbours.

I would also like to extend my gratitude to Harry Spiridakis and Ted Pandel for their generosity in talking to me about Bruce Haack, their late friend. Their website proved to be a valuable resource.

Most of all I would like to thank my wife, Darlis, and daughter, Darlana. Without their love and patience, this project would never have been finished. This book is as much Darlis' as mine. She spent countless hours transcribing interviews and proofreading copy. Ghost towns are her passion. When we married in 2001, it had to be in Nordegg. Best decision I ever made.

About the Author

Johnnie Bachusky is a national award–winning journalist who has explored hundreds of ghost towns across western and northern Canada since the late 1990s. He has written dozens of ghost-town and heritage-related articles for newspapers and magazines in Canada. Johnnie is also the author of *Ghost Town Stories: From Renegade to Ruin along the Red Coat Trail* and *Ghost Town Stories of BC: Tales of Hope, Heroism and Tragedy*. His heritage photography has been featured in national and international publications, and he has been consulted and featured in many television and film documentaries. As well, he is the co-creator of three acclaimed websites about ghost towns in Alberta, Saskatchewan and British Columbia, as well as the heritage photography site Silent Structures. His photography of pioneer wooden grain elevators is also featured on many websites, including Grain Elevators of Canada. He lives with his wife, Darlis, daughter, Darlana, and his three cats and hound in Red Deer, Alberta.

More Great Books in the Amazing Stories Series

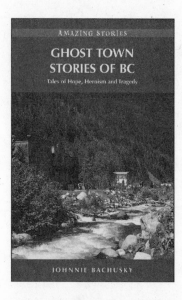

Ghost Town Stories of BC
Tales of Hope, Heroism and Tragedy

Johnny Bachusky

(ISBN 978-1-894974-73-8)

In the late 19th and early 20th centuries, dreams of wealth brought waves of opportunists to British Columbia. Some of the communities they built disappeared over time and today are almost forgotten. Johnnie Bachusky introduces readers to some of the fascinating characters and once-thriving towns that have faded into the past.

Also by Johnnie Bachusky:

Ghost Town Stories: From Renegade to Ruin Along the Red Coat Trail
(ISBN 978-1-551539-92-8)

Visit www.heritagehouse.ca to see the entire list of books in this series.